Your Pony Book

Tineke Bartels-De Vries
and Egbert van Zon

Your Pony Book

How to ride and care for the pony

CITADEL PRESS
Secaucus, New Jersey

First American edition, 1982

Copyright © 1979 by W. Foulsham & Co. Ltd. All rights reserved. Published by Citadel Press, A division of Lyle Stuart Inc., 120 Enterprise Avenue, Secaucus, N.J. 07094. Manufactured in the United States of America.

Library of Congress Cataloging in Publication Data
Bartels-DeVries, Tineke.
  Your pony book.
  Translation of: Het ponyboek.
  Includes index.
  Summary: Text and photographs explain the proper care and training of a pony.
  1. Ponies — Juvenile literature. 2. Horsemanship — Juvenile literature. [1. Ponies. 2. Horsemanship] I. Zon, Egbert van. II. Title.
SF315.B3713 1982   636.1'6   81-21628
ISBN 0-8065-0794-2 (pbk.)   AACR2

CONTENTS: Page

Foreword   6
What you need to know first of all   7
Understanding a pony   13
The pony at grass and in the stable   18
Grooming is half the battle   25
See to it that the pony looks neat   29
Plaiting of the mane and tail   33
Bandaging and protection   37
The saddle, the bridle and their care   41
Saddling and unsaddling   47
Mounting   54
Dismounting   57
Good posture and seat   59
How the pony moves   66
Sitting and rising trot   70
The aids: learning to talk to your pony   74
Exercises in the saddle   83
Exercises without the pony   89
Index   96

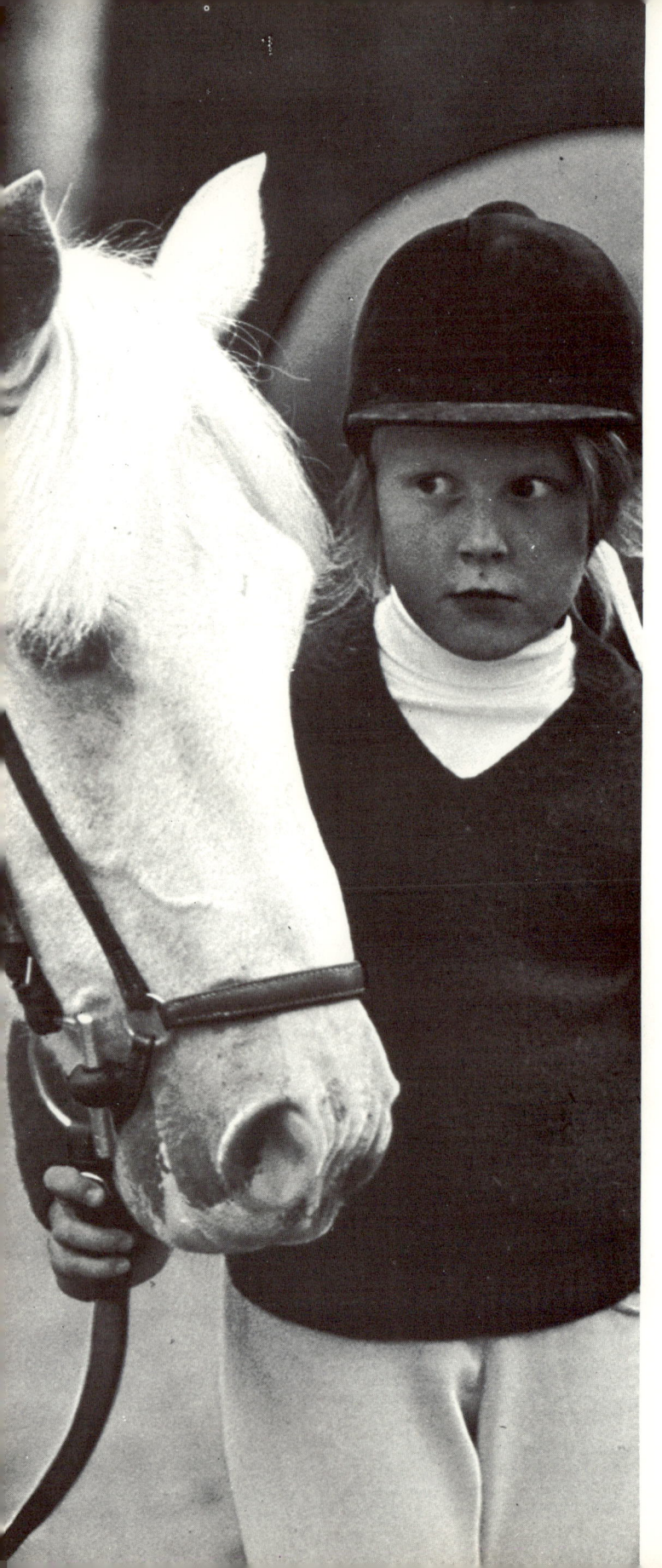

Foreword

Pony-riders should feel fortunate that *The Pony Book* has been published. Both the layout and the clear and simple descriptions make it an equestrian book which is pleasant to read and easy for children to understand. Parents who are thinking of buying a pony for their children would do well to read this book first for it will benefit both pony and rider, as ignorance can often be the cause of serious mistakes. I can thoroughly recommend this book to all who wish to practise or teach pony sports.

What you need to know first of all

There are a whole lot of things that you need to know before you start riding a pony. We are going to deal first with the appearance and a number of important features of the pony. This photograph names the important parts of the pony which you must know. Take a good look at them, and then we shall look at the way some parts of the body and organs work.

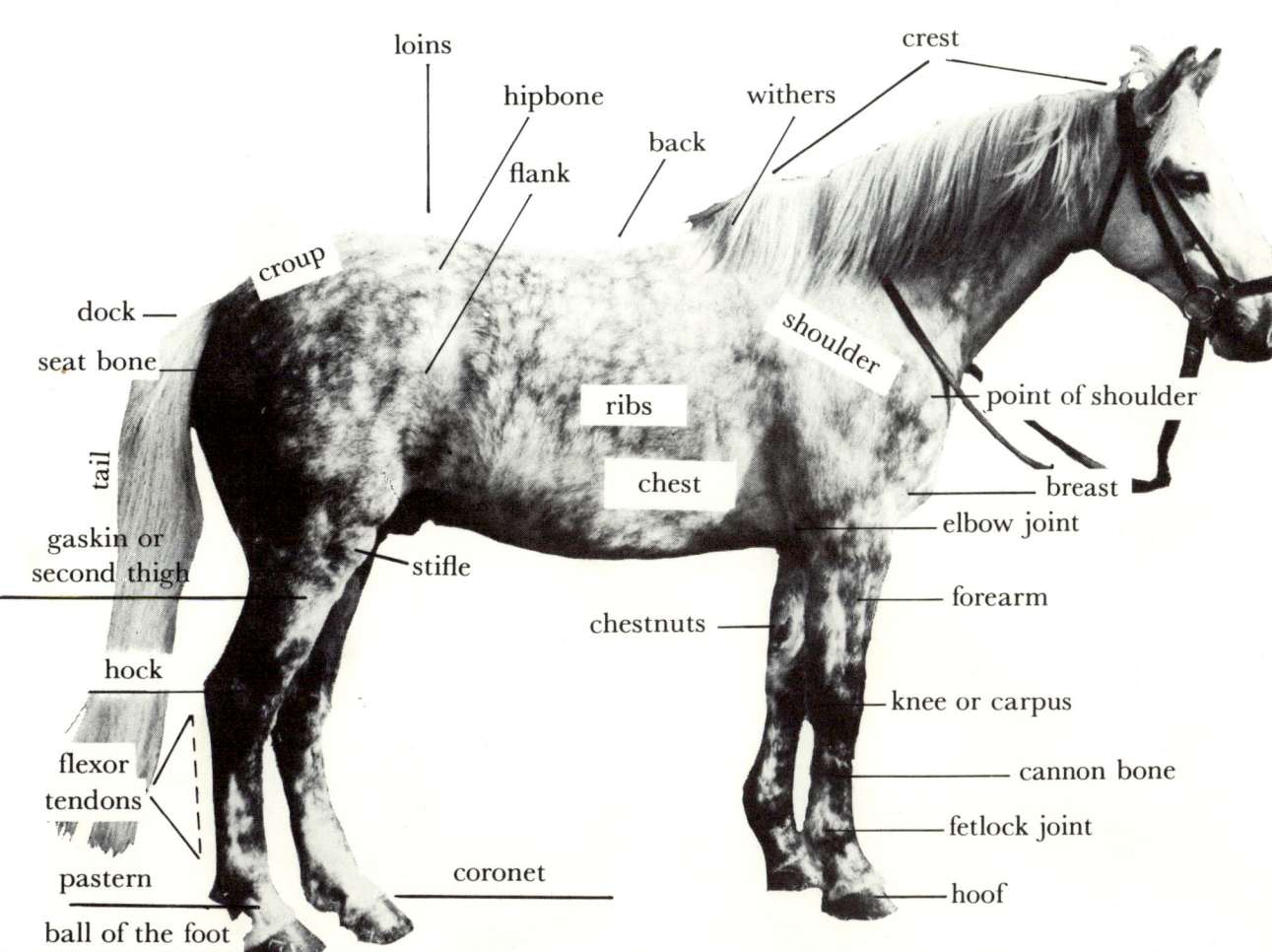

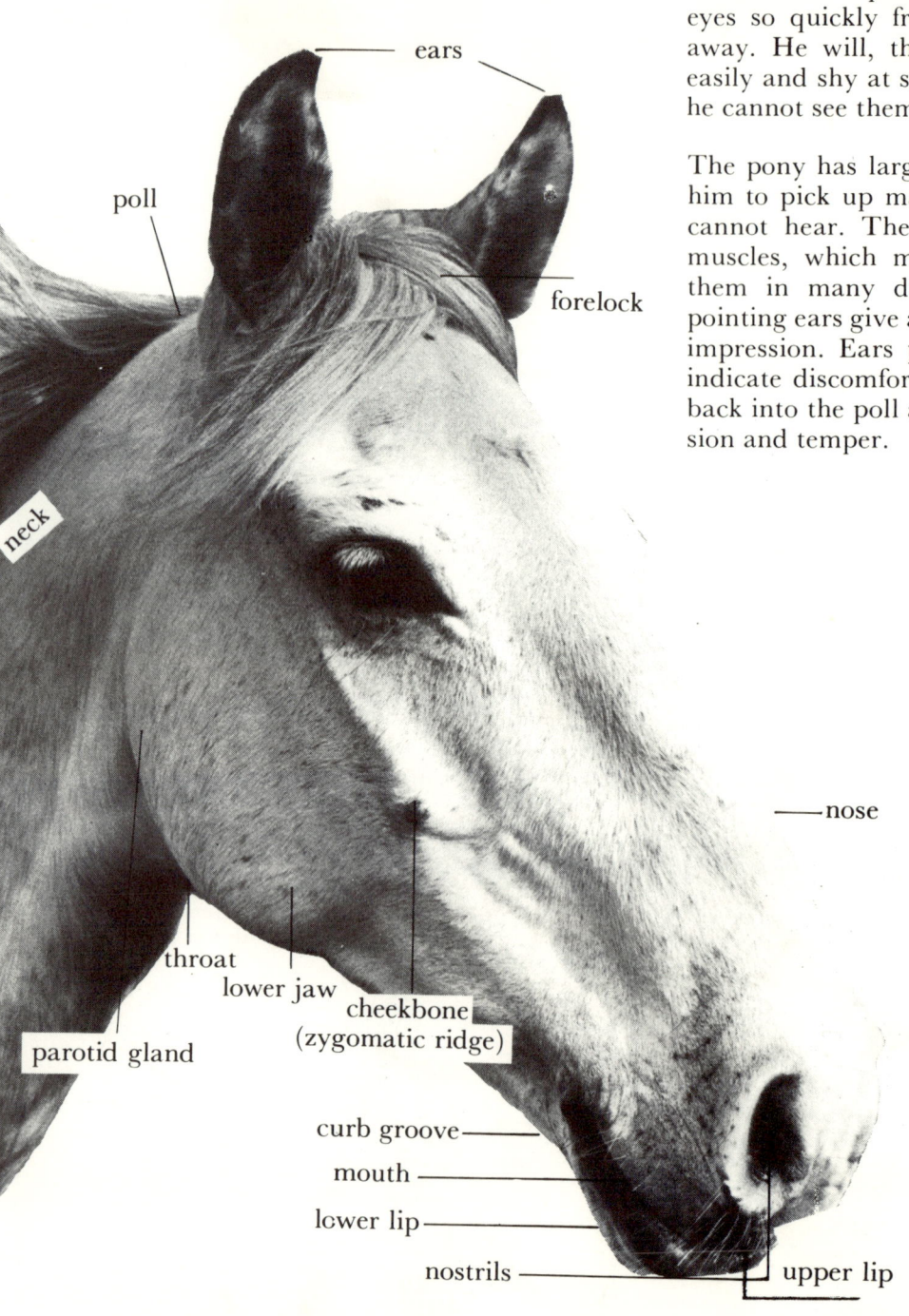

The eyes of a pony, unlike ours, are set in the side of the head. As a result, the pony has a wider range of vision than we have for he can see both ahead and to the side. A pony cannot adjust his eyes so quickly from close up to far away. He will, therefore, take fright easily and shy at small things because he cannot see them immediately.

The pony has large *ears* which enable him to pick up many sounds that we cannot hear. The ears have various muscles, which means he can move them in many directions. Forward-pointing ears give an alert and friendly impression. Ears pointing backwards indicate discomfort or pain. Ears laid back into the poll are a sign of aggression and temper.

The nose is for smelling, among other things. A pony has almost as good a sense of smell as a dog. For example, he will be reluctant to pass a slaughterhouse because, to him, it has an unpleasant smell. The nostrils must be large because they are needed for breathing – the pony cannot breathe through his mouth. Around the nostrils, on his lips and chin, are tactile ('feeling') hairs; these hairs are clearly visible in the photograph. They help the eyes in sensing close objects and they should never be cut off.

The mouth is important for picking up food. The pony is a herbivorous animal; that is, he eats grass, and he also has a sweet tooth. In his mouth he has incisors and molars; with his molars the pony grinds his food, with circular movements, also using his tongue. There is a space between the incisors and the molars called the 'bars'; this enables the rider to put a bit in the pony's mouth. You can tell the age of a pony from his teeth. Just like us, he first has milk teeth which later make way for permanent teeth.

In this photograph we can see clearly the jaws of the pony: they differ in size in different breeds. The area behind the jaws must be large enough to allow the jaws to flex easily, helped by a supple poll (the part just behind the ears) and also to provide room for the parotid gland. The function of the parotid gland is to produce saliva and it can produce many litres of saliva a day. If this gland is constricted, the pony will be in pain and will be difficult to handle.

If we compare a pony to a bridge, then his spinal column forms the arch from which the rib cage, which contains the internal organs, is suspended. In this comparison, the four legs form the piers of the bridge.

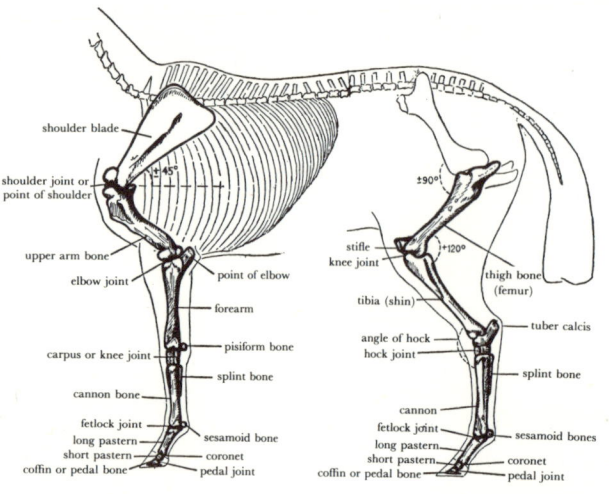

The propulsion, or movement, starts from the hindquarters and is transmitted by the muscles to the lumbar, thoracic and cervical vertebrae. The hindquarters can be compared to a locomotive pushing a row of carriages. You can see from the pony's shape that he was not born to carry loads. Human beings have given him that job. That is why we must patiently teach young ponies to put up with a rider's weight. The muscles of the back must be very well developed to help the spine to bear the weight of the rider and to absorb shocks. If we ask too much of the pony, he will not complain of backache, as people do, but he will hold his back stiffly; as a result his movements can no longer be supple and we shall not be able to sit comfortably on him.

As riders we must use the driving aids to bring the hindquarters forward. We shall then have a pony with a springy back, who walks with his nose slightly forward, and who is free in his movements – rather than a poor pony who is wrongly forced to bend his head and neck. You can see the correct way of producing this effect in the photograph.

The hind legs of a pony are firmly connected to the barrel via the pelvis and are the 'motor' of the pony. The front legs are attached only by muscles to the barrel. All the joints of the hind leg are bent – the hip, the knee (the stifle) and the hock joints. This contrasts with the front leg, where the knee joint is straight. As a result, shocks are absorbed better in the hindquarters than in the forehand; the front legs have to put up with more than the hind legs.

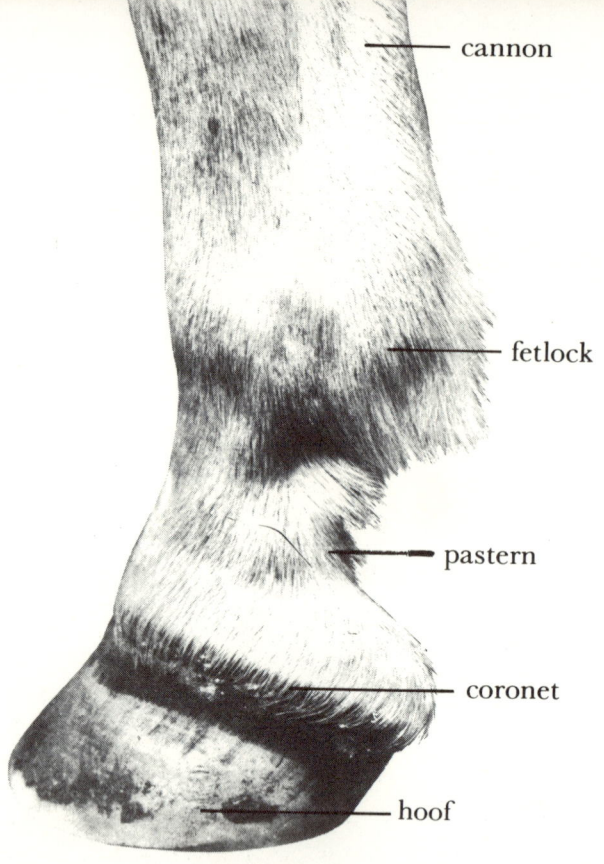

From the knee and from the hock joint downwards, the four legs of the pony are similar. In the photograph you can see, in succession: the cannon, the fetlock, the pastern, the coronet (the transition from the leg to the hoof), and the hoof. Let us take a close look at the pony's hoof.

We find in it a sensitive part – the fleshy 'leaves' – surrounded by a hard, insensitive part. The insensitive outside of the hoof can be divided into three parts: first there is the horny wall, which is what you see when the pony's foot is on the ground – it grows out of the coronet, just like a nail from a finger; the second part is the sole, which is on the bottom side of the foot and grows out of the sensitive tissue inside the foot – nails or other sharp objects can pierce the sole, crippling the pony if they touch the sensitive part; the third part, the frog, is important because it helps to absorb shocks.

In the photograph you can see three clefts, the central and lateral clefts of the frog, into which a great deal of dirt, such as animal droppings, can penetrate. Because of this the feet must always be picked out well. We shall deal with this later.

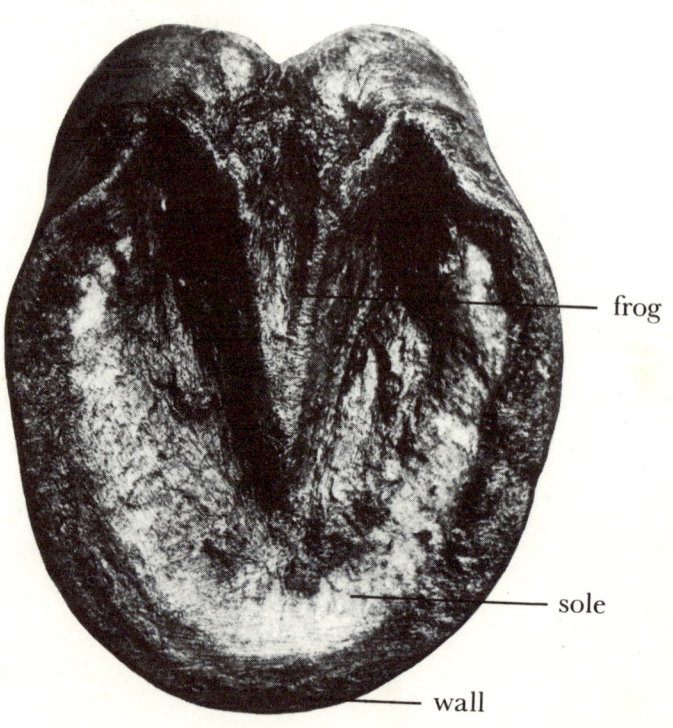

Understanding a pony

Having dealt with the physical features of the pony, we shall now turn our attention to the workings of his mind. In order to learn to ride, and to be able to handle ponies well, you must know what sort of animals ponies really are. Like horses, they used to be wild animals, who sought refuge by running away from everything that frightened or hurt them. You must always remember this, for it will often help you to understand a pony's behaviour.

A pony you have hurt by pulling too hard on his reins will run away, because his instinct tells him to. So you must not then pull even harder, but try gently to regain his trust. You must be able to understand a pony's instincts, then you will be able to use this knowledge in training him. If you go against those instincts, you will never form a good team with your pony. So you can never deal by force with situations like the one in this photograph.

A lot has been written about the intelligence of horses and ponies, but whether you find them intelligent or not, one thing is certain: ponies have very good memories, and they are cleverer than horses. You can make very good use of that memory when training, but it can also be a disadvantage. Once you have taught a pony to do something wrongly, it is very difficult to correct. So beware of teaching bad habits! You must try to be as consistent as possible with a pony, not friendly one time and ill-tempered the next. Always speak to your pony in the same way, always approach him from the same side (the left), always give him a gentle pat on the neck as a reward, and always give him identically worded commands if you want something from

him. Never be rough or become agitated when you are dealing with ponies, but, above all, do not spoil them too much. Spoiling ponies with lumps of sugar and other sweets only makes them tend to bite.

Apart from being a wild animal, the pony is also a gregarious creature. In the past, ponies lived in herds, as in this photograph, and each one always had his place in the 'pecking order'. Each herd had a leader, and in your dealings with your pony you must try to make your pony accept you as a sort of leader. Never let your pony become the boss, or you will not make much progress with riding. We have already said that the pony is a creature of habit and that you must make use of this when teaching him new things. But you must never demand too much of him at once; if you do ask something new of your pony, do it persuasively. Furthermore, you must always take plenty of time over teaching your pony, you must always remain patient and, above all, you must never lose your temper. Bad temper is the very worst attribute of a rider. If you lose your temper, you only make the pony uncertain and afraid, you break the relationship of trust and the pony will want to shy away from you.

Always remember that you get a far better result from reward than from punishment; and if you do have to punish, do not overdo it. A pony has a very good memory and he will remember an unreasonable punishment for a very long time.

There are fixed rules for handling your pony, and you must know them well. First of all, when tending your pony, never make any sudden movements or noises. When leading the pony, walk beside his shoulder, always lower the reins over his head and hold on to them, close to the bit, with your right hand. Put your forefinger between the two reins. Hold the end of the reins with your left hand.

The pony is a creature of habit. Once he has learned something wrong, it will be difficult for him to unlearn it. So make sure that you do everything right from the start; and this means that you must be very familiar with the normal techniques.

Standing still is one of the first things which a pony must learn. You cannot begin early enough with this. Standing still is important for grooming (brushing, picking out hooves), but later on the pony must also be able to stand still properly during a dressage test. It may sound silly, but standing still has to be learned. You must take your time in teaching this. You must speak kindly to your pony at the beginning, when he has stood still for a few seconds; initially do not make him stand still for too long. 'Do not expect too much' is the golden rule of early training. If the pony wants to move again before you do, give a tug on the headcollar or the rein and say clearly; "Whoa." Vocal aids are very important, but make sure that you always use the same words!

Moving on command in the box is also important. When you go into the box, you must be able to make the pony go anywhere you want. With a click of the tongue, you must be able to make him go forward, and with the command "Back", he must step back of his own accord. You can teach him all this. With patience, you can convey to him from the beginning what your intentions are. A reward in the form of a carrot is always a good idea. But do remember that it is always wrong to reward too much and, in the same way, to punish too much!

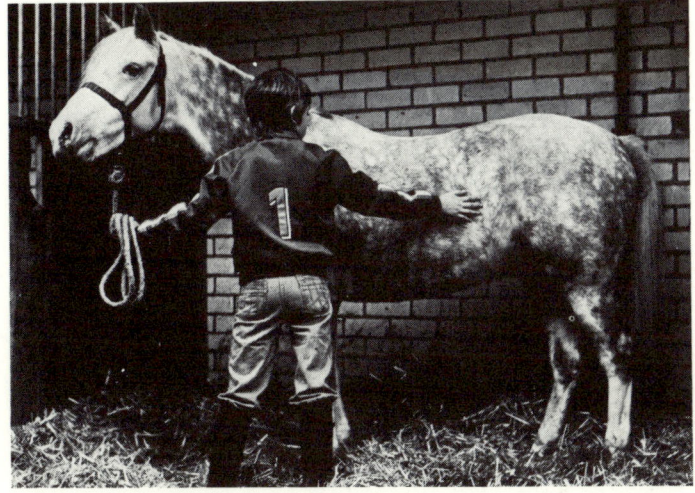

When you take your pony into or out of the stable, always walk in front of him on the near-side and look over your shoulder to make sure that he does not bump against the edge of the doorpost with his hindquarters. If this is very much of a problem, you can walk backwards in front of your pony, so that you are looking straight at him.

If a pony bumps himself often, it is because he is afraid of the door. So try and put him at ease, and reward him each time he goes through the door.

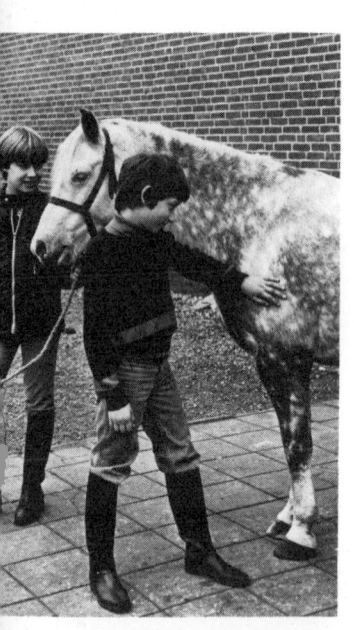
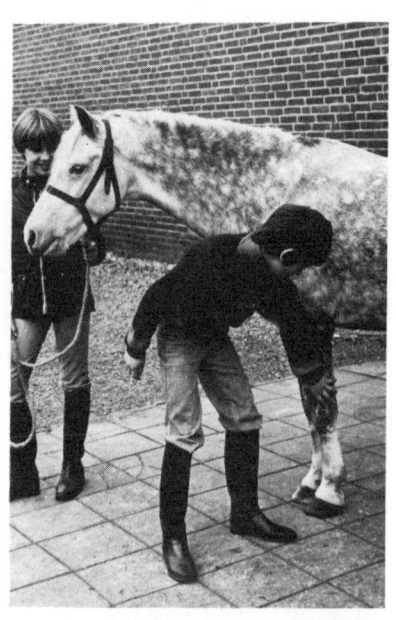

When you walk round a pony, always keep your eye on him. If at all possible, never walk behind him, even if you know him well. If you do have to walk behind him, first place your hand on his rump, slide it along the tail and take hold of the tail below the dock. Only then should you walk behind him. Also, when you have to lift up his legs, begin by placing your hand on the pony to reassure him. Stand close to him and let your hand drop down to the leg. Then squeeze the tendons and say "Foot" or "Up" (make sure you always use the same word). Try not to lift the hind leg too far.

With young ponies, you may have to press with your shoulder against the pony for him to allow you to lift his leg. When putting on a headcollar or bridle,

approach the pony from the front, with the headcollar over your left forearm. When you do it for the first time, make sure that you have a lump of sugar or a carrot in your left hand and then, when the pony tries to get hold of the sugar, stand by his head. When the pony has the sugar in his mouth, slip the headcollar over his nose, and you will then easily be able to place the headpiece behind the ears and buckle it up.

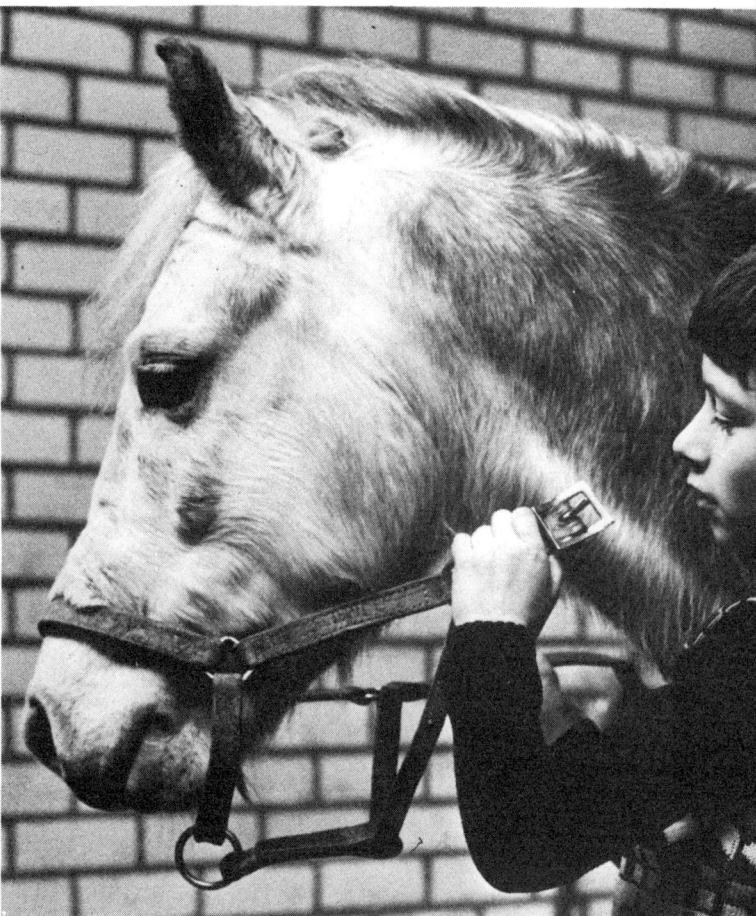

The knot you use to tie up horses and ponies is shown in this drawing.

When you lead your pony in public, you should always walk on the nearside. When turning you must make sure that your pony stays on your right, so always turn to the right!
You will observe at shows that the experienced 'model grooms' never turn to the left.

17

The pony at grass and in the stable

There are various ways of keeping a pony. You can leave him outside, you can keep him in a stable, or you can combine the two by leaving the pony outside during the day and putting him into the stable at night (or vice versa in the summer, because of flies, etc.). The most natural thing is for the pony to stay outside. He will lead a fitter, healthier and happier existence for he will be getting enough exercise and will eat more naturally. He will also be less susceptible to afflictions such as colds and lameness. The other side of the coin is, however, that the field is usually not as close to the house as the stable, and if there is a lot of rain, it will be wet and nasty for him. Besides, there are some ponies who are difficult to catch, so you may often have to exercise patience. You must not expect a pony that is outside all the time to be in top condition and to give you great performances. If you do, then he must be brought into the stable more often.

Let us now look at how a good field for ponies should be equipped. A pony who is outside all the time needs at least an acre of good grassland. As shown in the photograph, the pony must always have clean drinking water and, if necessary, must be able to stand in the shade. An open-sided shelter gives ideal protection against wind and weather.

You must make absolutely sure that there is good fencing. It is cruel to keep a pony behind loose and low-hanging barbed wire. Just think of what could happen if the pony hits out at a fly or wants to follow a passing horse and catches his leg in the barbed wire! It is best for the fencing to be of wooden sections or iron railings. It must be high enough to stop the pony from jumping over it. Another possible type of fencing is plain wire: it must be as taut as possible – preferably electrified, so that the pony gets a harmless shock if he touches the wire.

Maintenance of the field is important. We know that the pony has a sweet tooth but he is also choosy: he will eat all the nicest grass and leave the rest, no doubt where he has left his droppings. So you must remove the droppings reg-

ularly from the field and, if possible, let cows or sheep eat up the grass which the pony has left. Allowing sheep or cows to graze there is also good for keeping the pony free of worms; both ponies at grass and ponies in the stable must be wormed regularly, using a worming treatment you can get from the vet.

The treatment can be administered in various ways, for example, by mixing the powder with a tasty morsel and giving it to the pony on an empty stomach. Never put it into his drinking water! The pony will not drink it. There are also treatments which you can squirt into his mouth with a syringe. There is no need for you to give worming treatments every month: four to six times a year is enough. When you get a new pony, you must give him a worming treatment, and if you find that he has worms (you will see them in the droppings), repeat the dose after six weeks.

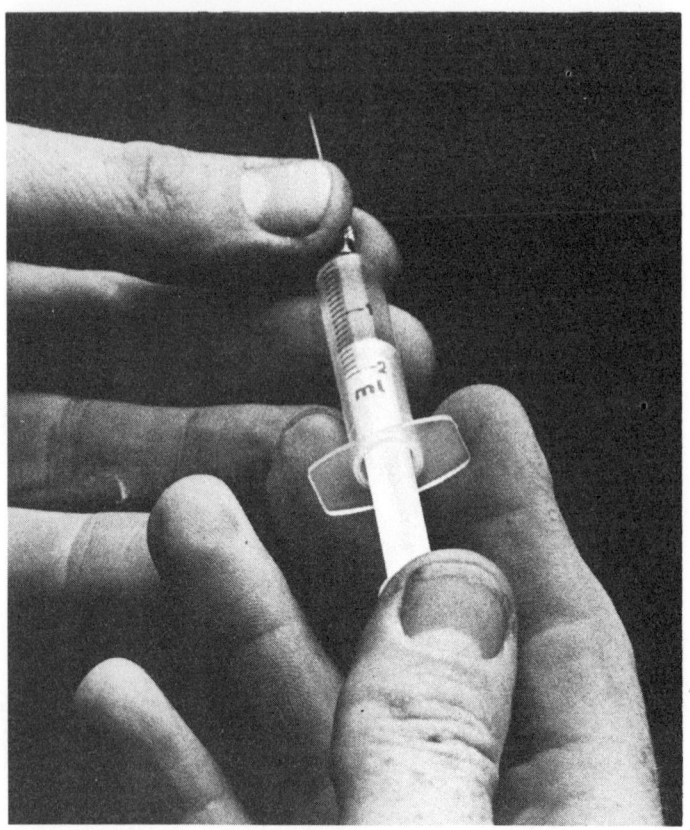

Apart from worming, it is important to have your pony vaccinated against influenza every year in the early spring, in order to prevent him catching it at shows and the like. Indeed, a vaccination certificate is compulsory at competitions. When you vaccinate your pony against influenza, you can also have him vaccinated against tetanus (a dangerous infectious disease). This prevents the pony from getting tetanus which can occur should a wound become infected through contact with animal droppings, manure, etc.

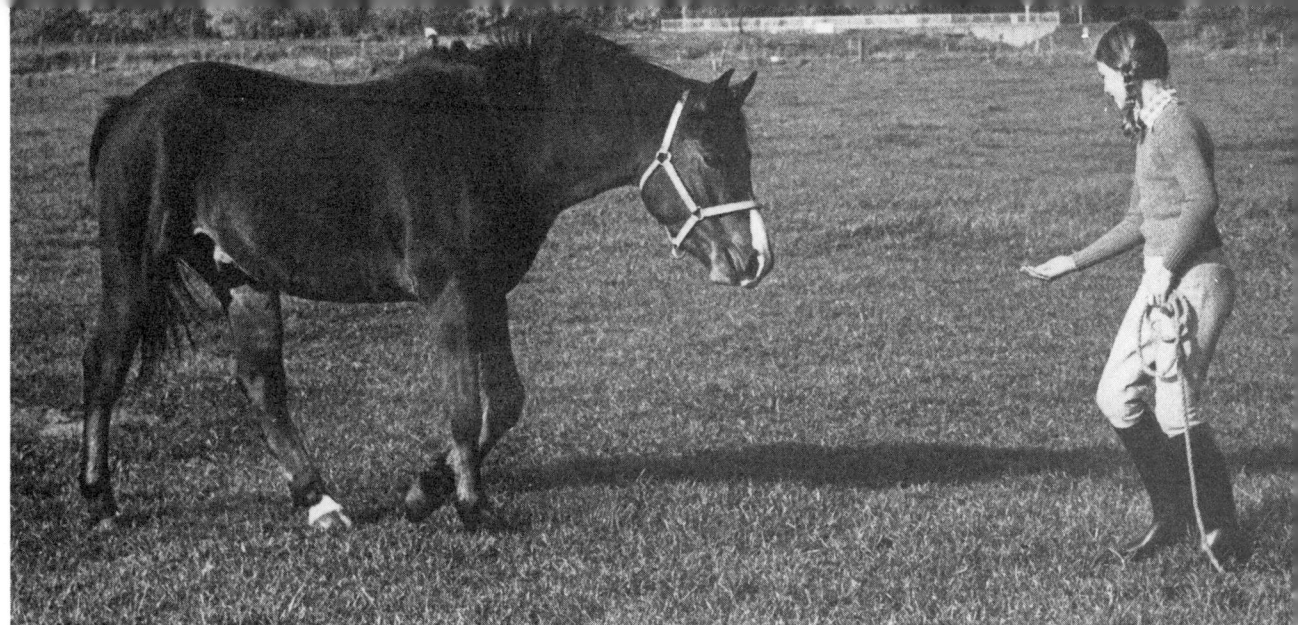

Two further points, before we take a look at the stable!
Always give the pony a titbit when you fetch him from the field. Then you will always be able to catch him easily when you need him. And when the pony is out in the open, he must always wear a headcollar, which should be comfortable at all times, preferably made of greased leather (cotton or cord shrinks after rain). Just imagine if he gets out of the field and he has no headcollar on! The only disadvantage is that there is a chance of the pony getting caught up somewhere by the headcollar.

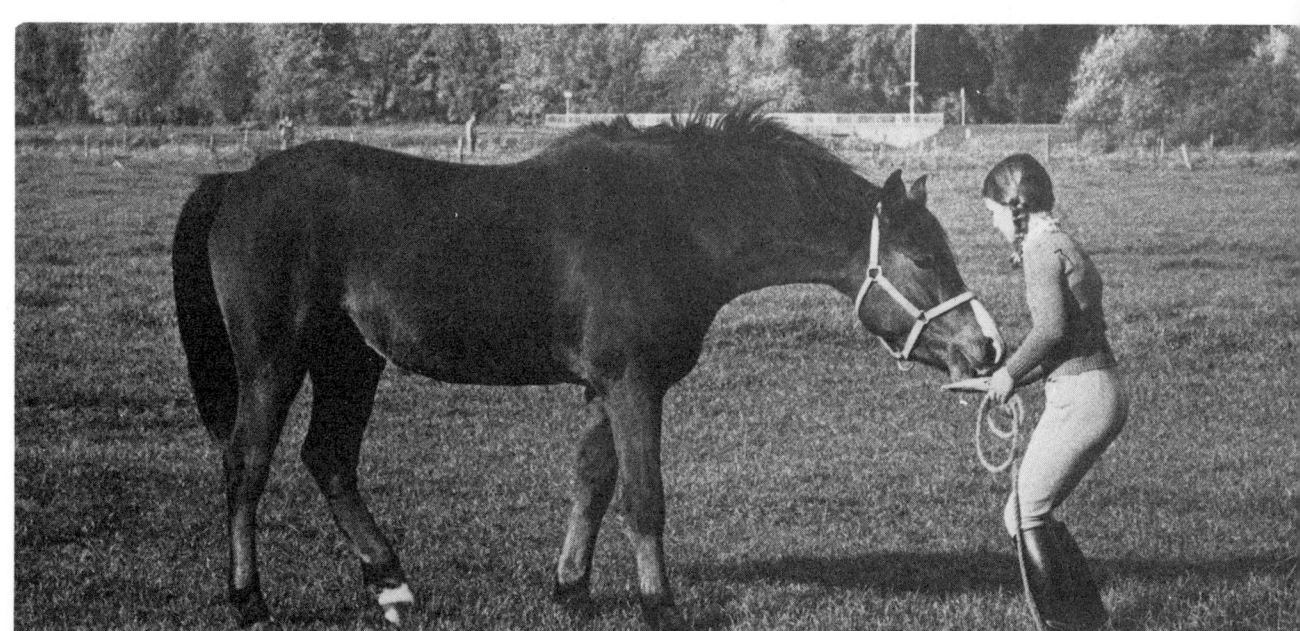

There are different types of stables: loose boxes and stalls. In a box – minimum size three by three metres (slightly larger than three by three yards) – the pony can move freely, so a box is better than a stall, where the pony is tied up. He is more likely to become bored in a stall, but it saves space. A stall must be greater in width than the height of the pony's withers, so that he can stretch his legs out when lying down. It is better to have the partitions between the stalls high to prevent the pony from biting or kicking his neighbour. You also find movable bails, like those in the photograph. They must hang so high that the pony cannot get his leg over them. These bails must be fixed so that they can be removed quickly in the event of accidents. With them, the ponies do have more space, but they can also annoy each other more easily.

This is how the knot should be made for fastening the bails between the stalls; it can be undone with one pull.

A good stable has adequate ventilation and drainage. It must not be too cold or too hot – the temperature is right if it is between 8° and 15°C. Make sure there is no draught – there must never be a draught in a stable. It must be kept clean and dry, and fresh water must always be available, so that the pony can drink when he wants. A pony drinks about 30 to 50 litres (50 to 90 pints) of water per day, depending on various factors such as his size, type of feed, etc. Nowadays, you may sometimes find automatic drinking bowls in the stable; these must be kept clean and checked regularly to make sure they are working.

As regards bedding, you must make sure that there is a thick layer of straw in the stable. All you need to do then is remove the wet and dirty patches and add fresh straw. It is a disgrace to find several heaps of dung when you go into the stable. So make sure that there is a good clean straw bed. The pony will then be able to rest well, and this will be all to the good. A dirty stable is bad for the pony's hooves. If too much dung and too many wet patches are left in the stable, the air will be ammonia-laden, and this is bad for the pony to breathe in, and bad for his eyes. Apart from the straw, you can also use wood shavings or peat moss as bedding. This may even be a good thing in the case of certain illnesses or if the pony cannot be cured of the habit of eating too much straw.

Finally, a look at the feed. The pony has a small stomach, so he likes to eat little and often when he is in the open air. You must make allowances for this when he is in the stable and feed him often with plenty of bulk food such as hay. The amount must be adjusted to the work he is doing, and it will also depend on the age and size of the pony. Shake out the hay well to get rid of any dust before giving it to your pony. Feed him at least three times a day at set hours. Your pony needs extra protein when he is working, so give him oats and pony nuts. Pony nuts have all the ingredients necessary to keep him fit and healthy. If you combine pony nuts with hay as the bulk food, these two feedstuffs will be sufficient when he is in the stable. A carrot now and again is a good thing.

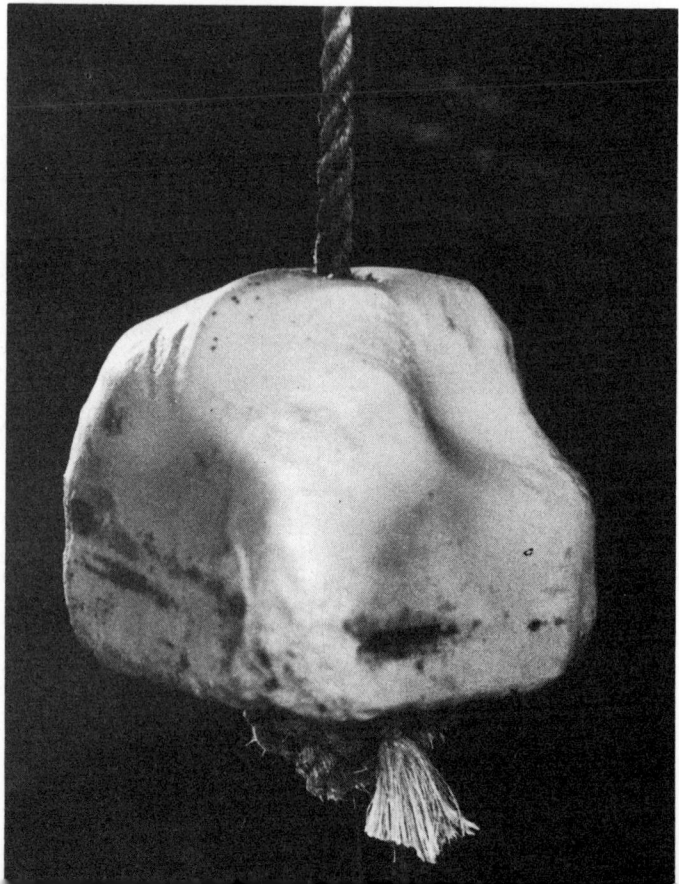

A pony at grass can be given some pony nuts as extra feed, depending on his size, the work he does and his age. Do not forget that a pony needs salt; some need more, some need less than others. You will find that a salt lick in the field or stable is appreciated.

Grooming is half the battle

Grooming is not carried out just to make our ponies look neat. Daily grooming is indispensable for the health of a pony who spends a great deal of time in the stable. In the field it is not necessary – indeed it is not a good thing – to groom a pony every day. A pony in the open sees to his own skin care by rolling on the ground, and he has help from nature in the form of showers of rain; but in the stable the pores of his skin can become clogged with excess grease, flakes of skin, dried sweat and dust. Brushing and massaging are also good for his circulation and stimulate the growth of skin and tissue.

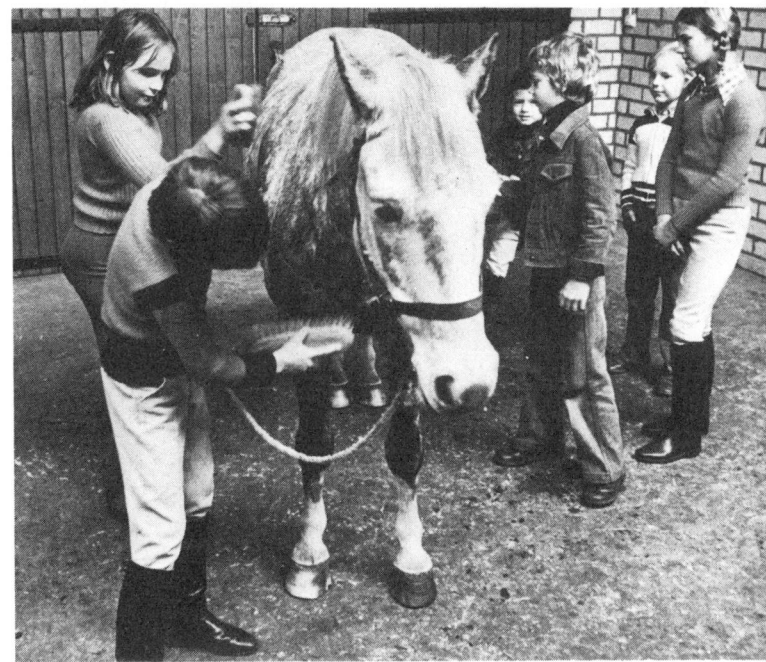

A full grooming kit comprises the following items:
1 a hoof pick for cleaning the feet;
2 a rubber curry comb for massaging the pony and cleaning the brush;
3 a dandy brush for removing the coarse dirt between the hairs;
4 a body brush for removing the fine dust from the surface of the skin;
5 a sponge for cleaning the eyes, the corners of the mouth and the dock;
6 a cloth for cleaning the skin and giving the final touches to the grooming;
7 a sweat scraper for removing sweat or water;
8 a mane comb for combing and pulling' the mane;
9 a brush for oiling the hooves and some hoof oil.

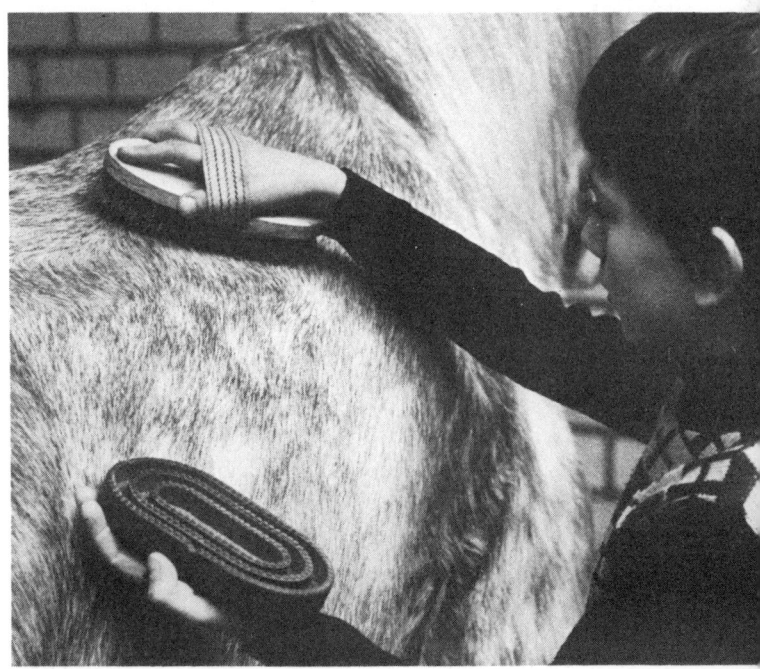

Grooming should always be carried out according to a fixed procedure.
Start with the hooves: pick them out with a fine hoof pick first of all. Then use the dandy brush to brush out the hard clods of mud and the coarse dirt. Using the curry comb (never the metal one, for that is used only for cleaning the brushes), clean the mane and massage the body, using circular movements. The curry comb should be regularly cleaned by knocking it out against the wall or the ground. The pony's head must be groomed very gently.
After the curry comb, you can use the body brush. You must keep the curry comb to hand, so that the brush can be cleaned regularly with it. After that, you can give the pony a shine with the cloth.

Remember: grooming is half the battle. Brush the head gently if there is coarse dirt on it. The eyes, nose and mouth are then cleaned with a damp sponge, after which the sponge can be used for the dock. Rinse it out well afterwards! When doing the head, do not forget the skin round the ears and underneath the forelock, for there is always a great deal of dried sweat there after riding. Like the rest of the body, the head is finished with a cloth. If you groom the head regularly and are very careful not to bang the pony's head with a brush or curry comb, you will find that he enjoys the grooming more and more; his trust in you will grow, and you will benefit from this when you come to put on the bridle and headcollar. Ponies who are a little 'head-shy' (who do not like having their head touched) can have their confidence restored by the daily grooming.

The tail is another matter. Many people say that you should not brush it too much if you want to keep it nice and full: and there is some truth in that. When you pull the curry comb, the dandy brush or the mane comb through the hairs of the tail, you will see that you pull a lot of hairs out at the same time. Therefore, you should not do this too often and that is why it is better just to remove the straws from the tail by hand when the daily grooming is being done. You can also wash the tail from time to time with a shampoo mixture in a bucket of water. You should only use the body brush on the tail if you are going to a show or competition, and carefully at that. You must take plenty of time for this and go through the tail with your hands, strand by strand, so that you can carefully brush out the tangled hairs.

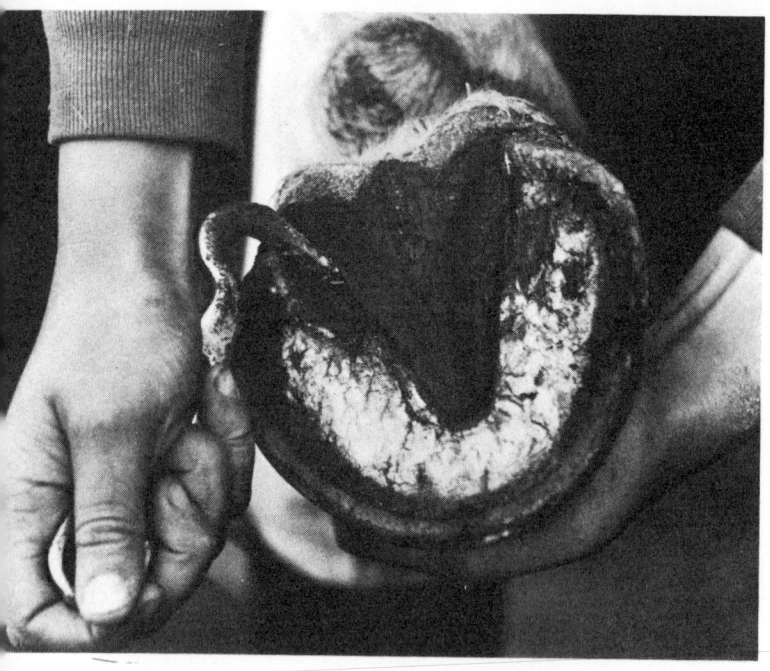

We have already talked about the care of the feet. Picking out the frog and the V-shaped clefts under the hoof is always the first part of any cleaning operation. But it is not enough merely to pick out the hooves during the daily grooming; it must also be done after working the pony, so that you can see whether any stones or, even worse, nails and the like have become lodged in the frogs. If your pony's feet are not healthy, the pony's whole health will suffer. There is a great deal of truth in the saying: 'No foot – no horse.'

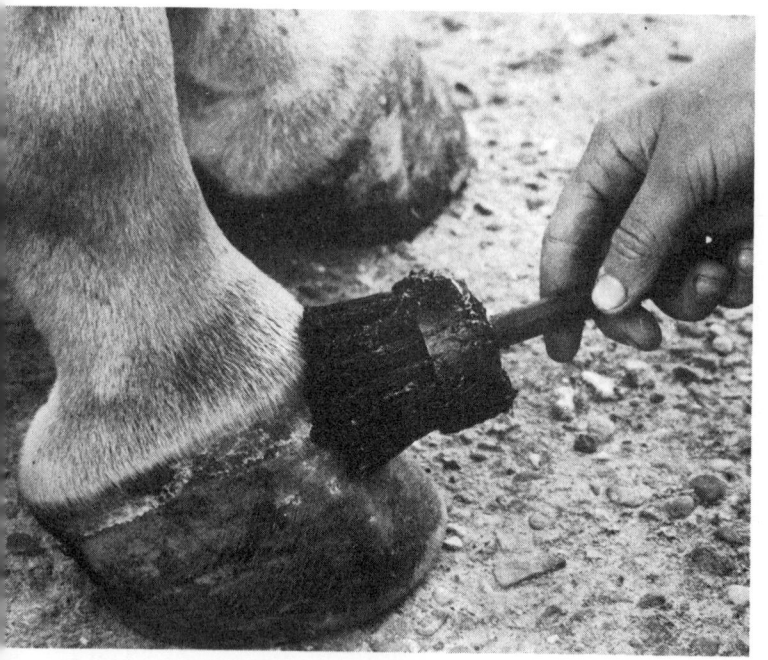

You must not only pick out the feet regularly, to keep them in good condition, but you must also see that they are attended to every six weeks by a farrier, even if the pony is unshod. You must remember, during grooming, that when you have picked out the hooves, you need to lave them with a wet brush. After that you can oil them with a special hoof oil for the purpose. This prevents the hooves from drying out too quickly and becoming brittle. Just oiling, without wetting the hooves, is not ideal either. If the horn of the frog becomes too soft, you should rub Stockholm tar, which you can buy from the saddler, into the bottom of the foot.

See to it that the pony looks neat

If we want our pony to look neat, we shall have to clip and trim him regularly. This means removing the untidy hairs from the legs, head, mane and tail. Not all ponies are clipped in the same way. For example, a Welsh pony or Fjord has its mane standing up, and on a Haflinger the mane and fetlocks must be kept as long as possible. So a distinction must be made between the different types of pony.

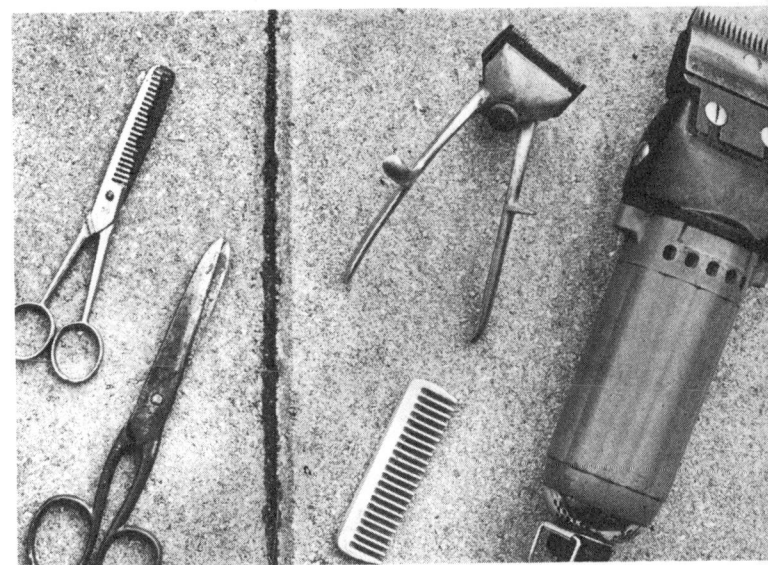

For clipping and trimming we need the following items:
- clippers (electric or hand clippers);
- metal comb;
- brushes;
- ordinary scissors;
- thinning scissors.

Let us now look at how we should clip the pony. Start with the legs. Using the clippers, clip away the long hairs above the coronet. If you do not have clippers, you can easily do it with scissors.

The fetlock, which is the tuft of hair low down on the pony's leg, must be clipped straight, to produce an angle. It is wrong to trim the fetlock in such a way that you get a curve. All the long hairs on the back of the cannon should be thinned out with thinning scissors. You must clip away the long hairs in the bulb of the heel, as in the photograph.

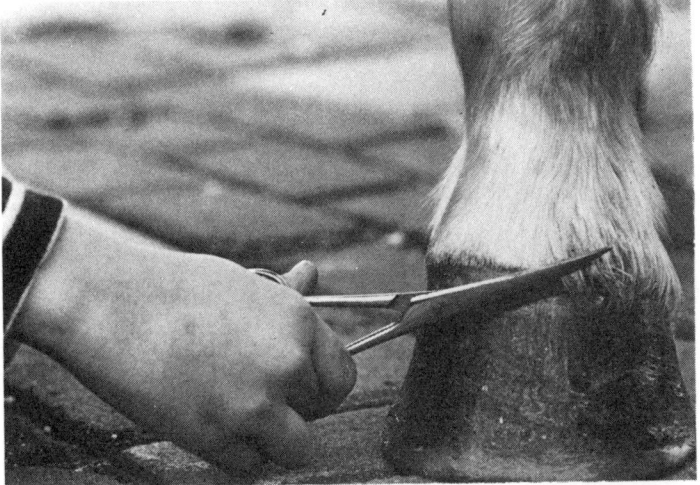

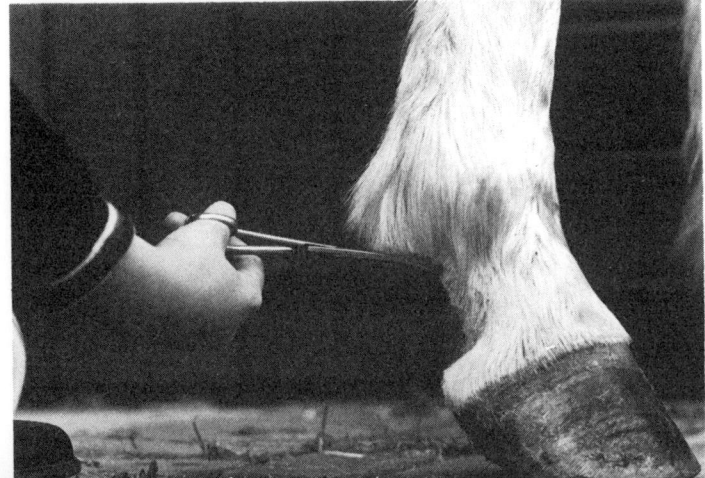

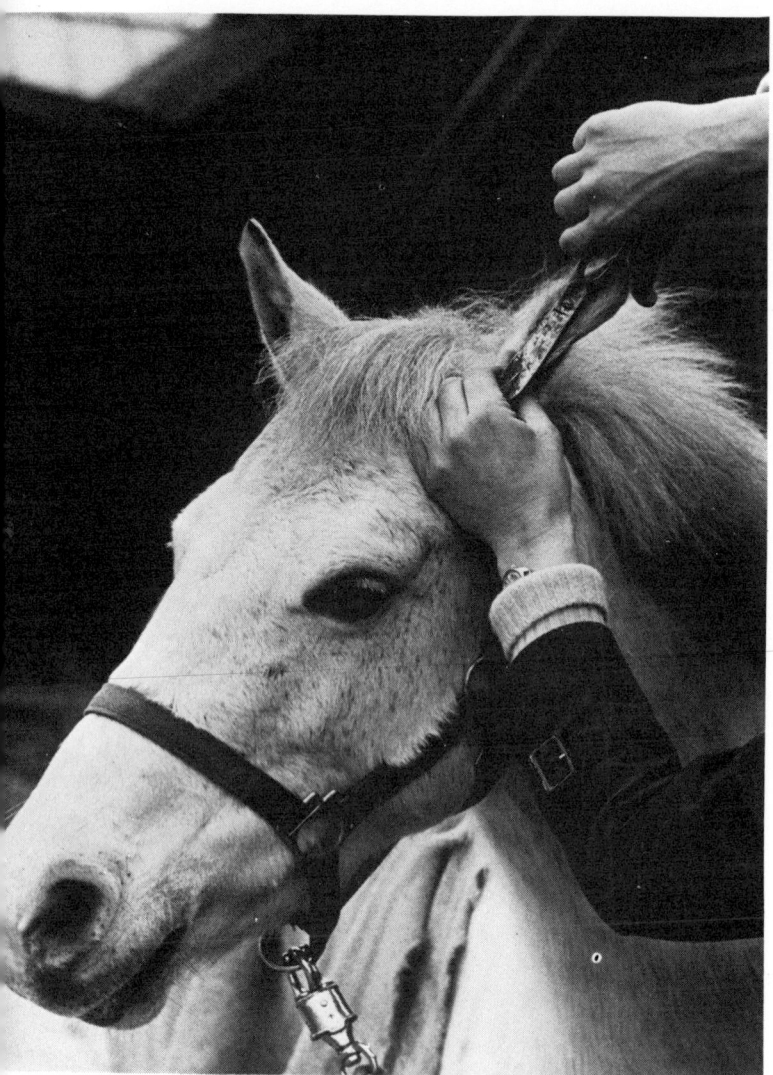

On the head you may trim away the long hairs on and between the lower jaws. Leave the tactile hairs on the nose and lips alone, for the pony needs them for sensing and touching, for example, when eating. Long hairs on the ears should be trimmed along the edges only. Press the edges of the ear together in your left hand, and with your right hand trim away the hairs standing out beyond the edge of the ear.

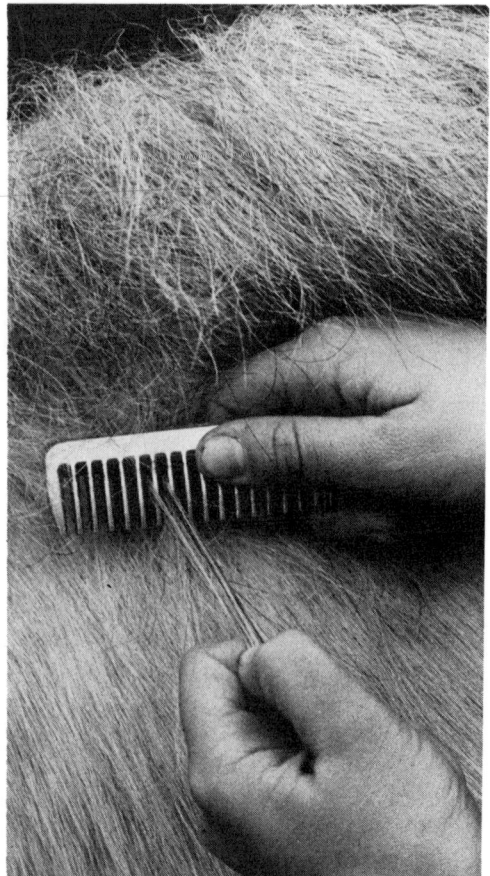

To tidy up the mane, you must carefully pull out the long hairs. Draw out the long hairs and push the shorter ones back with the mane comb.

Then twist the long hairs once round the comb and give a slight tug to pull them out. This should give you mane hairs which are all the same length, about a hand's breadth. You can also just thin out the mane in this way if it is very thick.

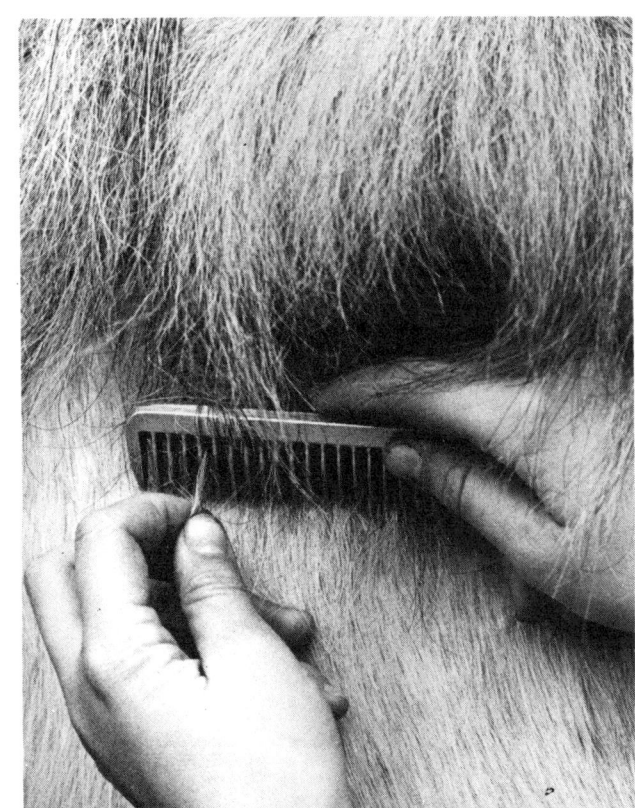

The hairs between the ears, where the headcollar sits, are clipped with clippers or scissors. Take off no more than about 4 cm (1½ inches).

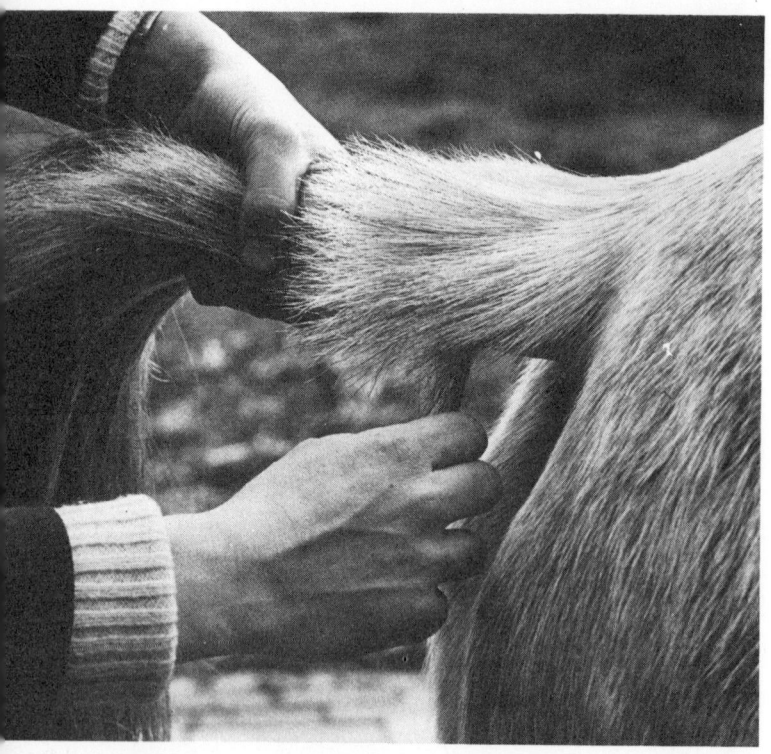

Finally, the tail. If the tail is too long or too pointed, you can shorten the point with the scissors. The length will depend on how the pony carries his tail. In general, it should be two hands' lengths below the hock. If you do not intend plaiting the tail at the top, you can pull out the hairs on both sides at the top by hand.

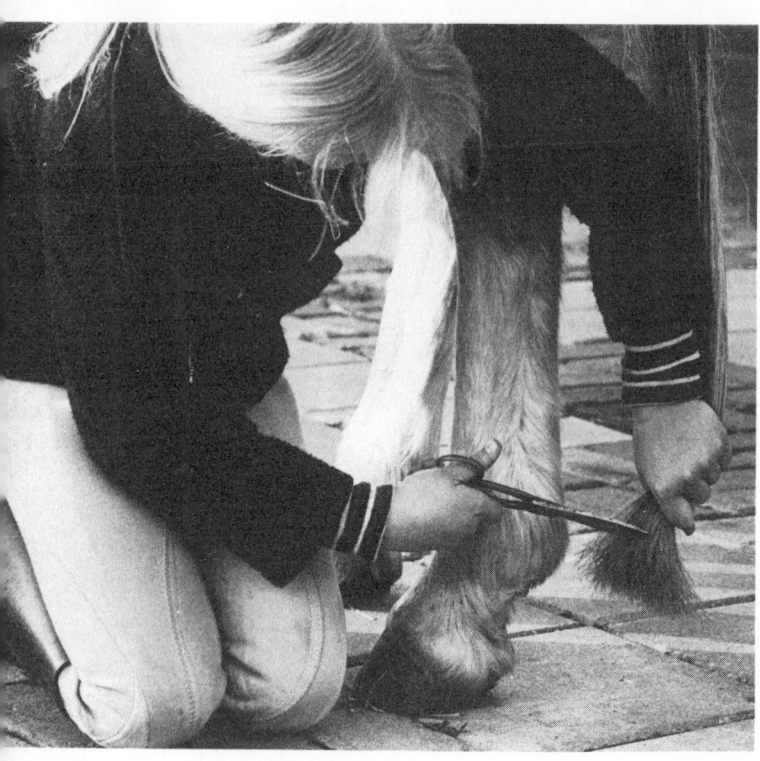

Plaiting of the mane and tail

If we want our pony to look nice at a show or competition, we shall in many cases have to plait the tail and the mane. Of course, this does not apply to all ponies! Think, for example, of Welsh ponies or Fjords – we have mentioned them already when we talked about trimming and clipping.
Begin by combing down the hairs on the neck, for the plaits must hang down flat when you have finished. Start at the top, near the ears, and damp the mane.

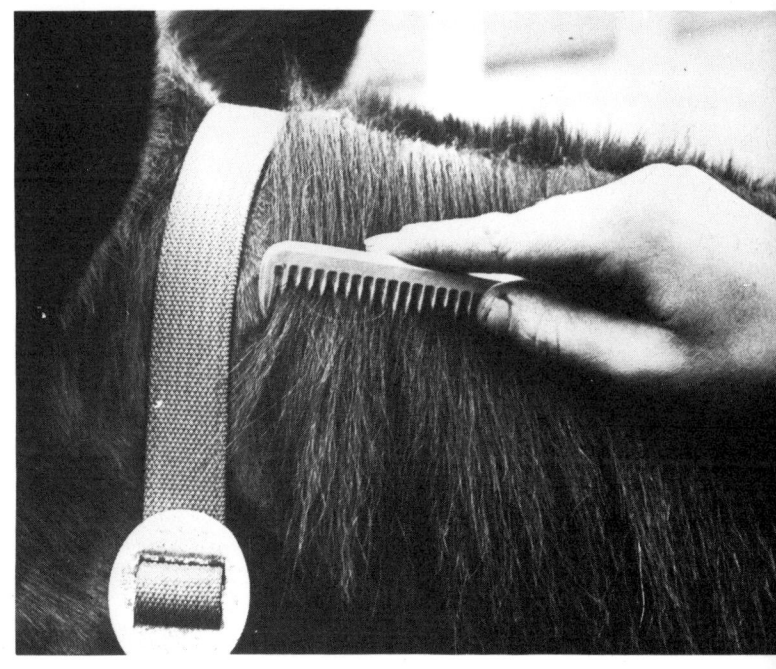

If you cannot reach that far, stand on a box or a bale of straw. Then take a strand of hair about 5 cm (2 inches) wide and divide it into three equal sections. Fasten the rest of the mane back with a clothes peg, so that it cannot get mixed up with the other sections again. Then plait the strands flatly and tightly against the neck until you reach the end of the hair.

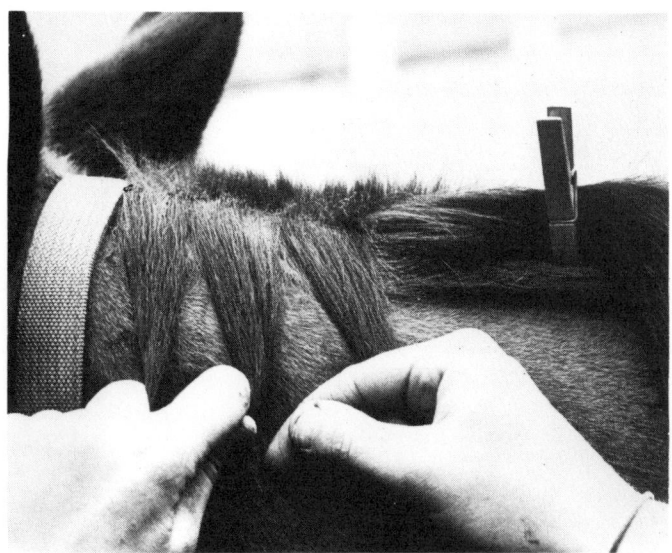
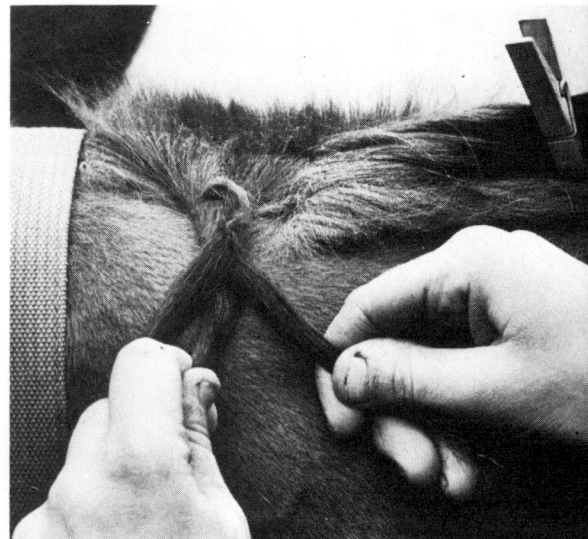

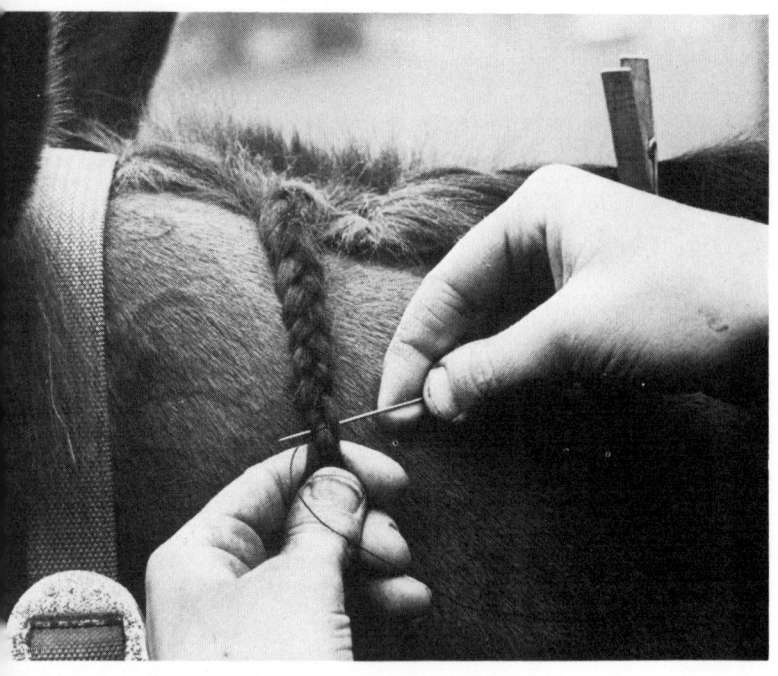

The photograph shows how you can finish off the plait with needle and thread, for binding up later. You can also do this in another way, for example, by fixing a rubber band or white adhesive tape at the end.

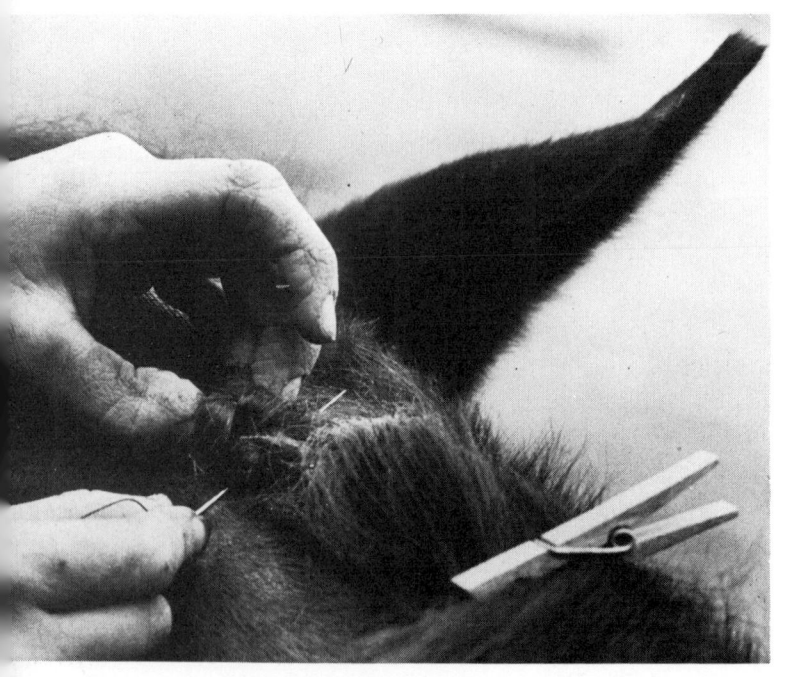

Finally, you must fasten up the plait. In the photograph this is done by turning it in, rolling it up and fastening it with needle and thread. This method is little used nowadays. With this method, no white adhesive tape is used on the plaits. The remainder of the plaits must, of course, be equally thick, long and tight, and they must be spread evenly over the crest to get a neat result. In this photograph the pony's mane is not plaited tightly enough. The plaits are not lying nice and taut against the neck, and they are tied up untidily.

This pony is tidier. Here, a tarred cord has been plaited in with each plait. Part of the cord remains hanging at the top of the plait, part is plaited in up to the end of the plait and fastened to the point, and the last part is left hanging. When all the plaits have been shaped in this way, they are then tied up one by one. The point of the plait goes underneath and the two ends of the cords are tied together round the double plait and trimmed off. Only then are the white adhesive tapes stuck round the plaits. The forelock may also be plaited, if desired.

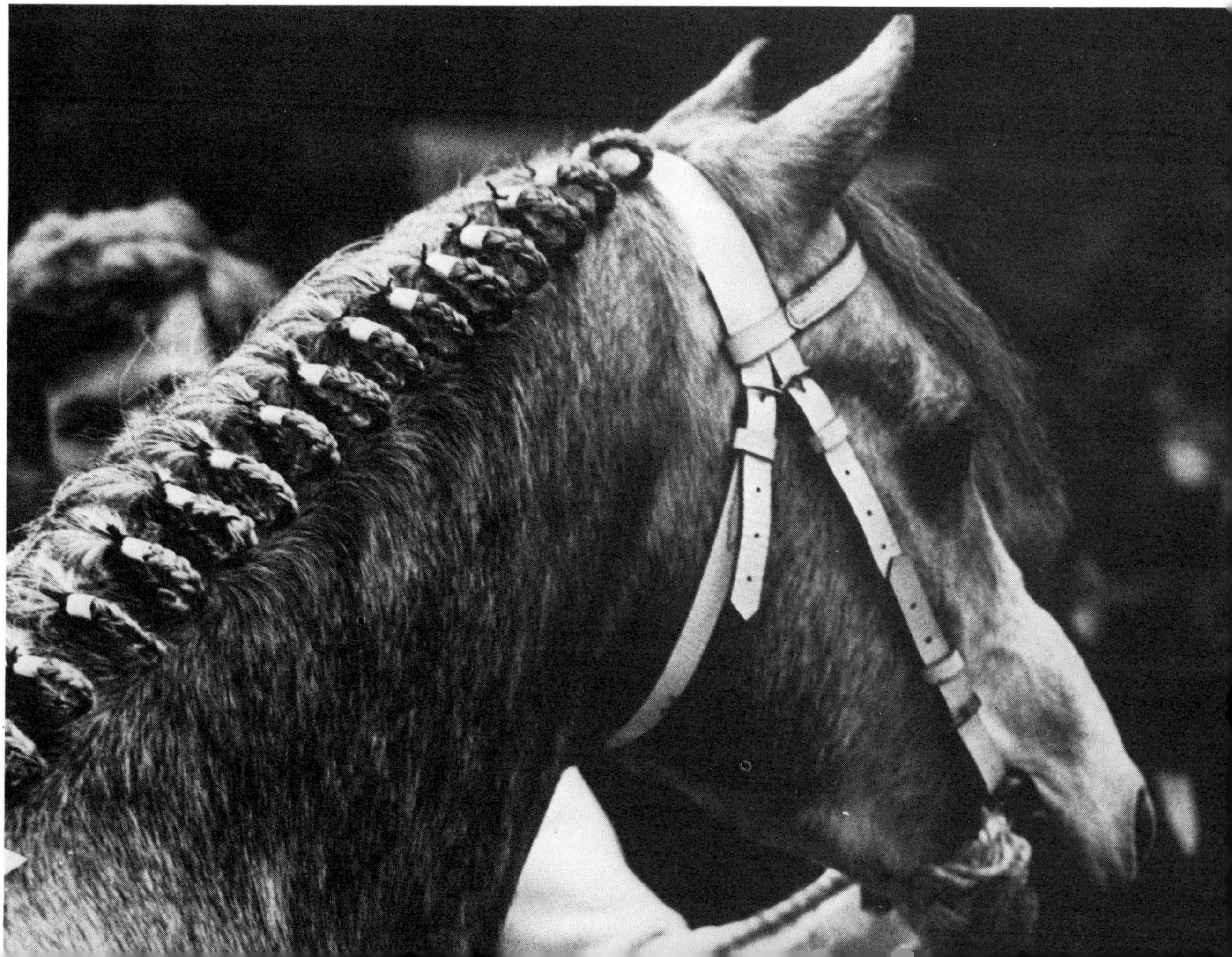

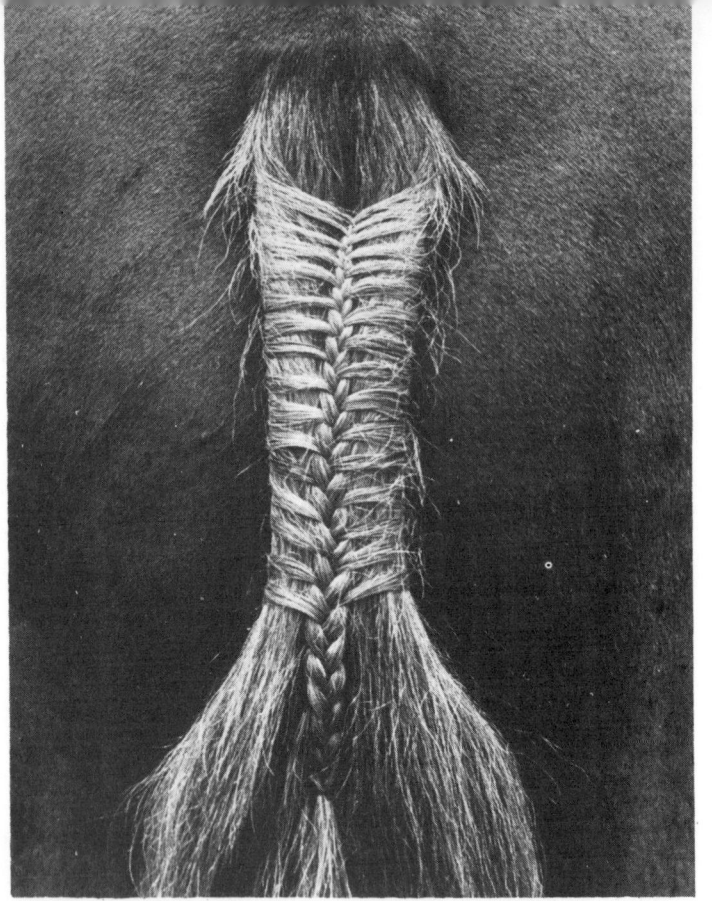

In this case you should plait the outermost hairs of the tail together over the dock for about 25 cm (10 inches). The hairs of the tail must be long enough for this, so they should not have been pulled out or clipped off. The plaiting must be fine. In the top illustration, unfortunately, the plaiting was started too low down, probably because the hairs were too short at the start of the tail. Take a small strand of hair each time and plait from the outside inwards, so that you get a plait in the middle over the dock. After about 25 cm (10 inches), just continue with the plait and fasten it off by putting a cord or elastic band round it. To give a good finish, you can tuck this part of the plait back up underneath all the rest.

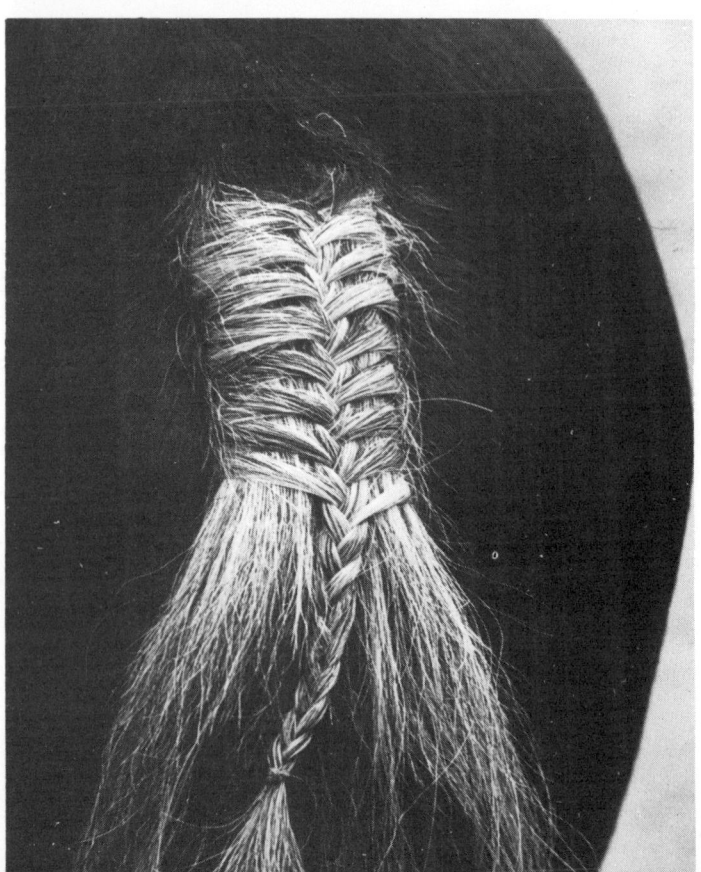

In this photograph the plaiting is not tight enough or fine enough. It was started at the right height on the tail, but it did not go down far enough. With the same effort it could have been much nicer. Make sure that you do not plait too tightly, for this may irritate your pony and he will carry his tail badly. Another more difficult method is to plait the tail by taking one of three strands through underneath – instead of over the top of – the other two. Here again, keep taking a new strand from the side until you are about 10 cm (4 inches) from the end of the dock. Then continue as described above. The plait now lies on top of the dock.

Bandaging and protection

Since the pony's legs are his most vulnerable part, and this is the first place where he can injure himself, his legs must be well protected. You can do this with all kinds of bandages and protectors. First of all, you must have woollen stable bandages. After a hard day's work, these will keep the legs warm and give them support. On a journey, they will protect the legs from shocks and knocks.

At competitions, and when lunging or doing work involving great demands on the pony's tendons and muscles, Gamgee tissues or cotton wool under elastic bandages should be put on for support. The pressure and support are then evenly distributed, since the cotton wool or cloth assumes the shape of the leg.

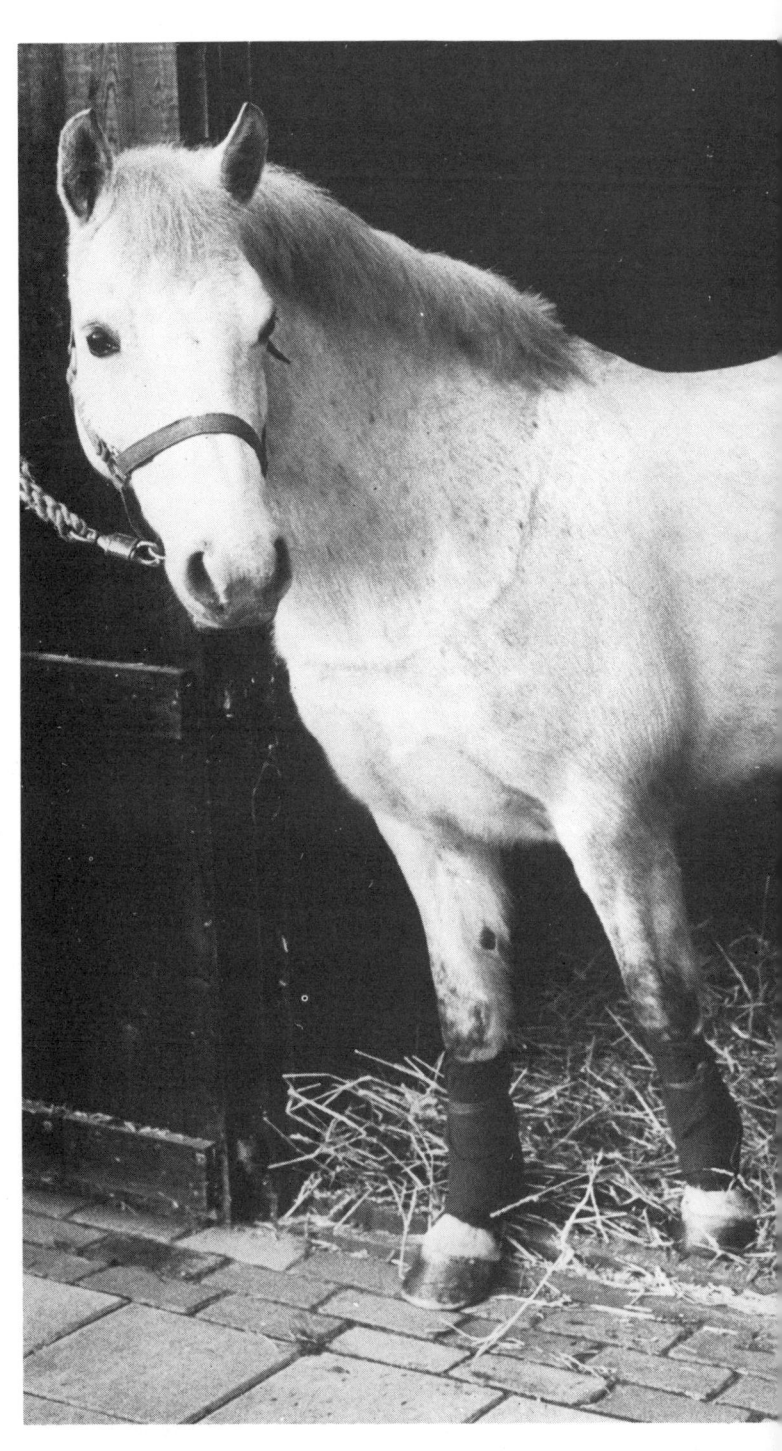

We are now going to look at how you put on a bandage. Begin by smoothing down the hairs. Lay the end of the bandage against the inside of the cannon, almost a hand's width above the fetlock joint, and then wind it to the left on the left leg (to the right on the right leg); repeat for the hind legs. So you work from the inside forward, out round the cannon, then go twice round, working downwards, at the same time tucking in the end of the bandage.

Wind well round the fetlock joint (not too low).

With stable or travel bandages, on the other hand, you go down below the fetlock joint, then up to just below the knee. The tapes must be tied very securely, with a knot on the flat outside edge of the cannon. You can use white adhesive tape to give extra hold. Carelessly applied bandages are dangerous! Think what could happen if the pony became entangled in bandages which had become undone!

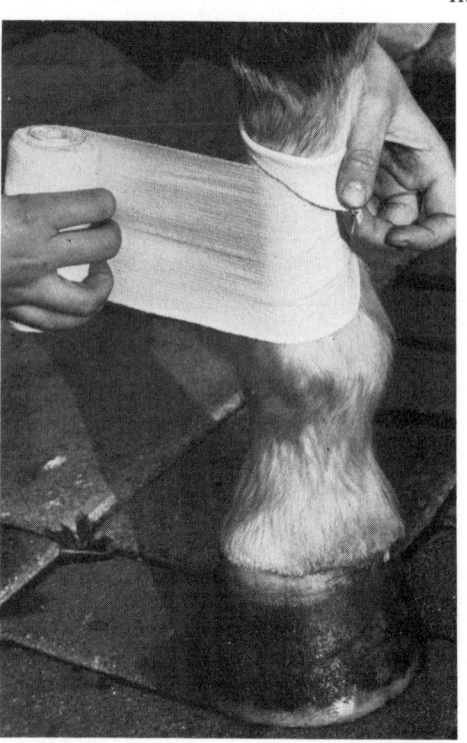

For competitions, jumping or cross-country riding, various types of leg protectors are used. In the photograph, you can see overreach boots, which protect the front feet if the hind hoof strikes the front hoof. The protectors worn by the pony in the illustration protect the tendons: they are a little too large for this pony. Other types are: tendon boots, brushing boots, knee boots and hock boots, to protect the cannon, fetlock joint, knee and hock, respectively.

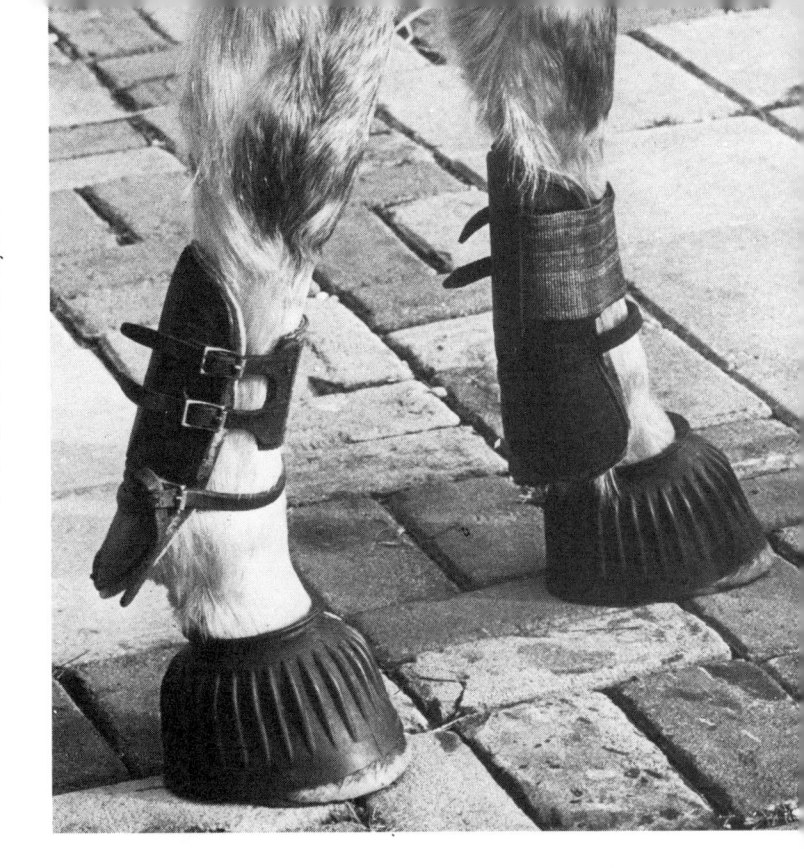

To protect the tail from chafing during travelling, you can put on a tail bandage. Start half way along the dock and work downwards, then go back up and fasten the tapes securely. You must not make the bandage too tight, or you will stop the circulation in the tail. Of course, you can also use a tail protector, which you can buy in riding shops.

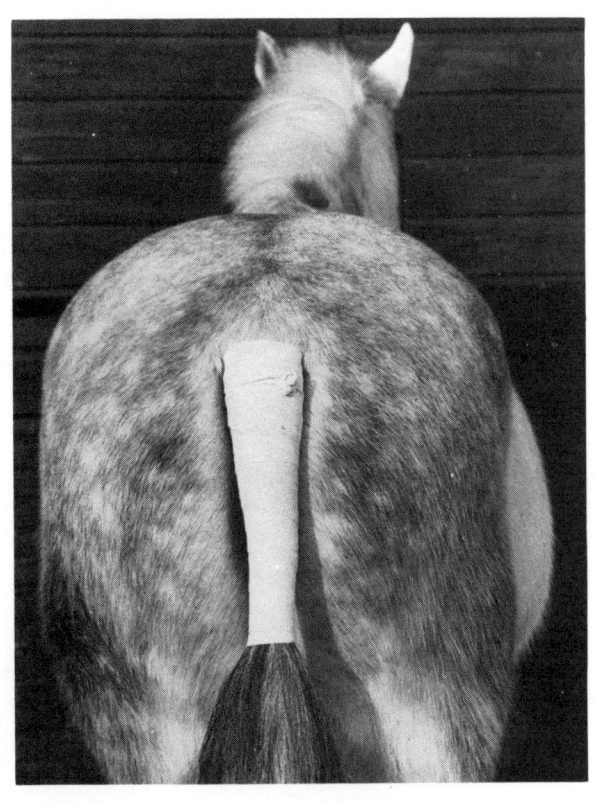

If you are going on a journey with your pony – in the horse box, to a competition or the like – then he should look something like the pony in the photograph.

You should wrap his legs up well with woollen bandages, having first put a blanket over him. You will need a loose girth, on to which you can fasten the tail protector. Underneath the tail protector there is a tail bandage. On the headcollar there is a rope with a safety snap hook or panic hook, which you must be able to undo quickly if necessary. Put a band round the top part ('the headpiece') of the headcollar. This will greatly reduce the chances of the pony knocking his head, and he will be less likely to be frightened of getting into the horse box. If you have knee boots, it is a good idea to put them on him as well. If you do all this, there is very little chance of the pony injuring himself.

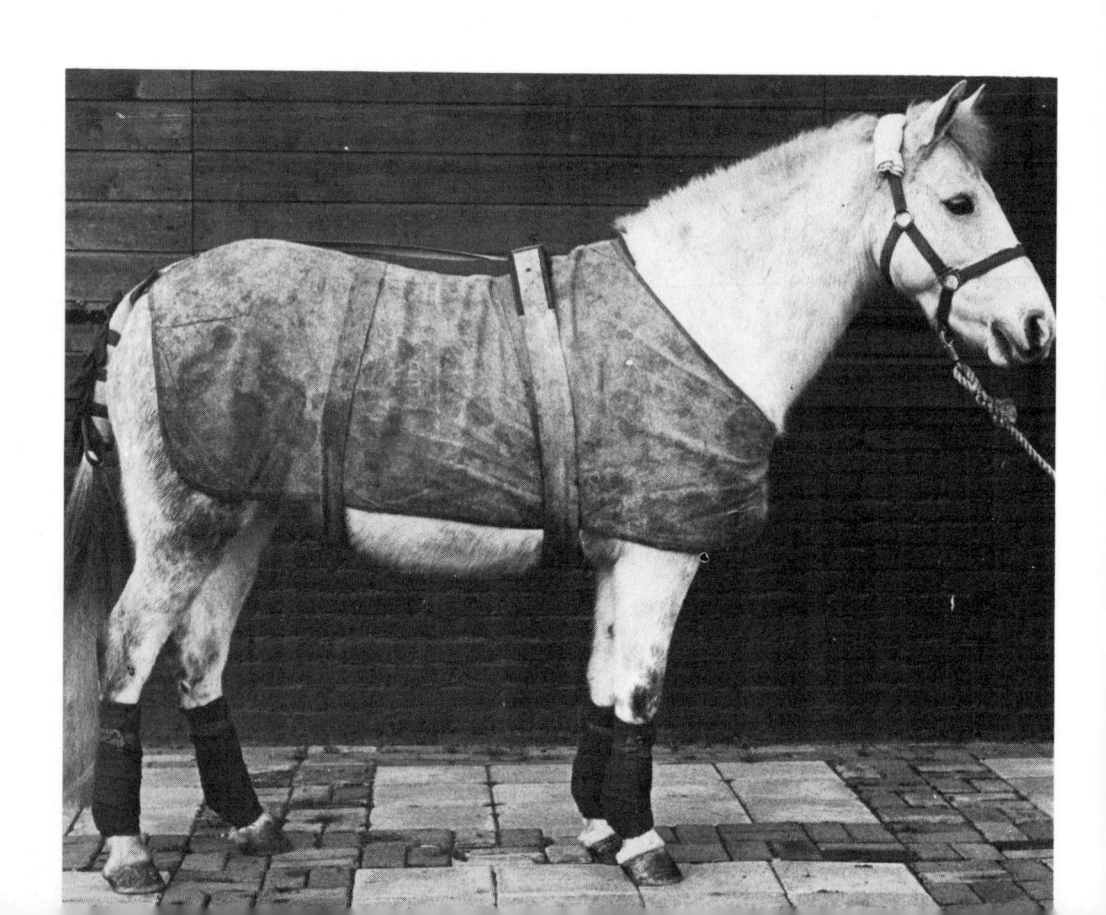

The saddle, the bridle and their care

You need both a saddle and a bridle to go riding. If you choose a good saddle, it will help you to become a good rider. A saddle must fit well on to the pony's back, but it must also be comfortable for the rider. A saddle which is dipped slightly will help you to stay well in the middle, at the deepest point of the saddle, so that you can keep your balance and follow the pony's movements. If the saddle is too broad, it will be difficult to keep your thighs flat against the saddle. The stirrup leathers must be fastened so that they do not catch your legs. Choose stirrup leathers and buckles which are not too thick or too heavy.

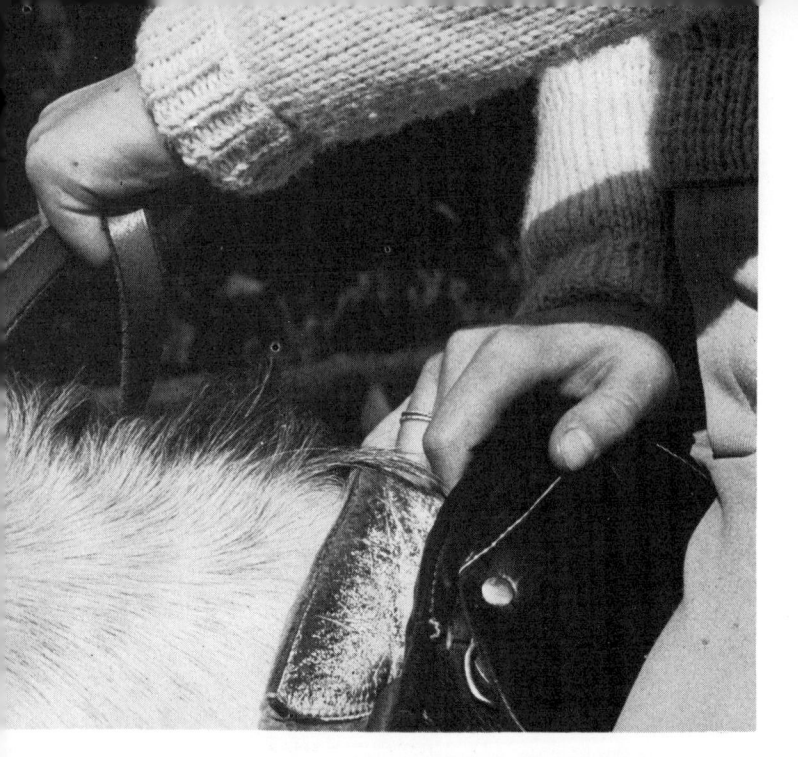

In order to prevent galls (bruises of the skin and underlying tissue), make sure that the pommel of the saddle does not touch the pony's withers and that the cantle does not press on his back; you should be able to see daylight through the saddle gullet.

The stirrups are attached by stirrup leathers – which should not be too thick or too wide (approximately 2 cm [1 inch]) – to the stirrup leather bars, which are provided with a safety catch. Never ride with the safety catch in the closed position as illustrated – this is very dangerous (this position is used only when the horse is led in hand).

Choose stirrups which are large enough, so that you can always get your foot out of them easily. They must not be too large either, or your foot could slip through them. Put a rubber tread in the stirrups to make it easier to keep your feet in place.

The saddle is fastened on to the pony by means of a girth. Make sure that you use the right size for your pony. Girths can be made of cotton and nylon, which you can wash, and of leather, which need to be well maintained – all girths get dirty very quickly from sweat and mud. Lay a numnah or saddlecloth underneath the saddle to protect it from sweat and grease and to protect the pony's back from galls. There are felt and cotton numnahs, the cotton ones are available in different colours and you can wash them easily.

The bridle plays an important part in guiding the pony and, like the saddle, it must be a good fit. This means that the bit must not be put in too high or too low, but in such a way that it wrinkles the corners of the mouth slightly. The bit hangs on the cheekpieces and can be adjusted there. As it rests on the 'bars', which are very sensitive, never use a sharp bit.

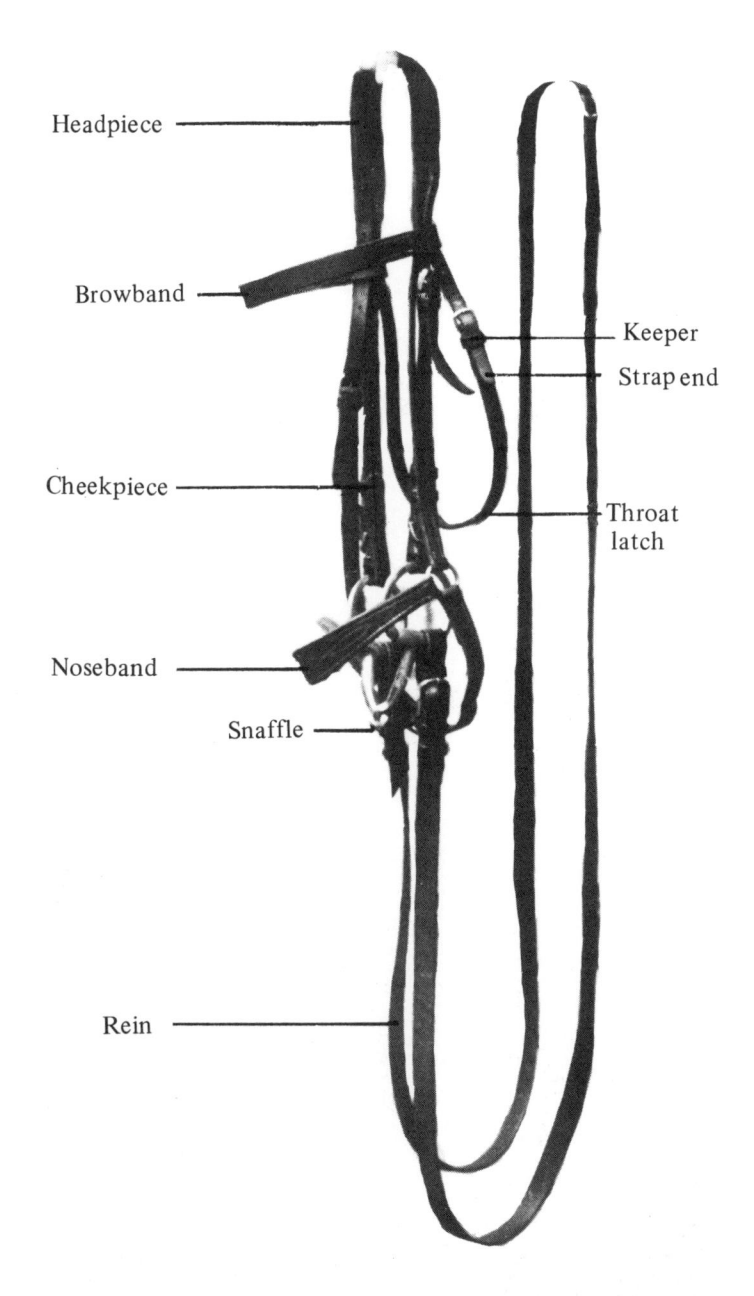

The reins are attached to the bit. Using them, the rider applies pressure to the sensitive bars, thus guiding the pony. There are various kinds of rein. First there is the plain leather rein, which you must use when riding in dressage competitons. Then there are various kinds of martingales and reins which do not slip through your fingers, for example, woven cotton reins, rubber reins and reins with stitched-on pieces of leather.

Never hang on to the reins; that is not what they are for! If your balance on your pony is still not good, use a neck strap. This is a simple (stirrup) leather which is fastened round the pony's neck, just in front of the saddle, and which you hold on to if necessary, to avoid pulling the pony's mouth.

A snaffle is used as a bit. This is a smooth, round bit which is usually (though not always) jointed in the middle. There are various types of snaffle: the wire-ring snaffle (which has the disadvantage that the pony can hurt himself – this seldom happens – if a piece of skin from the corner of the mouth gets between the rings of the bit); this cannot happen with either the egg-butt snaffle or the D-ring snaffle (where the rings are D-shaped). An even softer bit is a rubber snaffle, both jointed and unjointed.

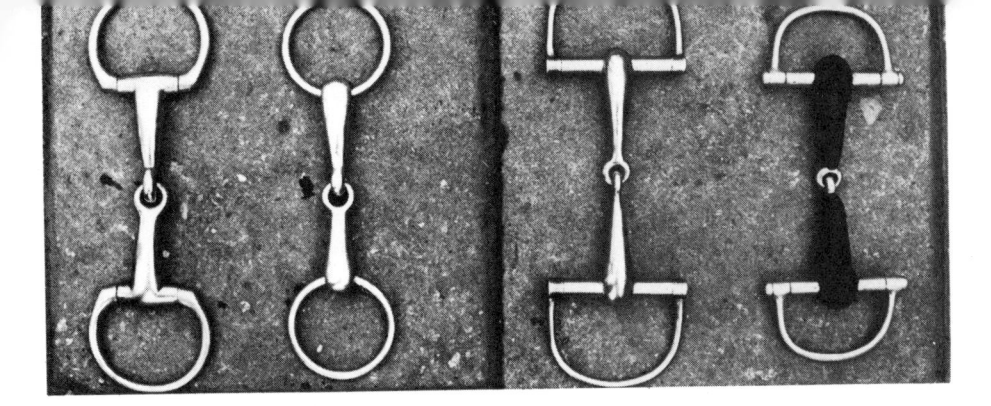

A dropped noseband may be used with a snaffle bridle. This noseband passes underneath the bit, as you can see in the photograph, while a cavesson noseband is fastened above the bit; with the latter, the pony can open his mouth more easily, with the disadvantage that he can free himself a little from the reins.

Usually we do not need any more tack than this. As a rule, the less tack you have, the better. However, nowadays there are all kinds of auxiliary reins. You can take this as a sign that the rider is pretending to be more expert than he is.

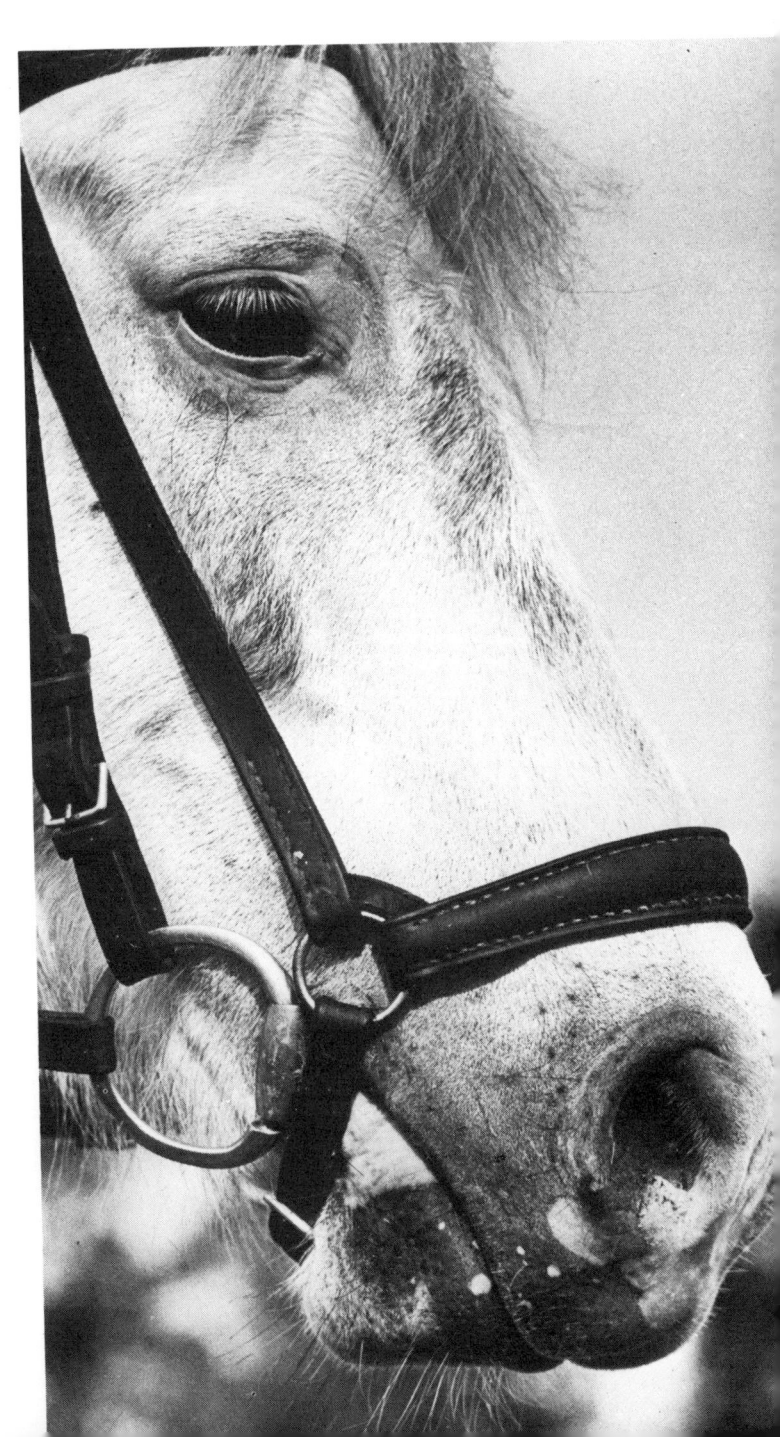

One auxiliary rein to which we have little objection is the martingale, where the reins run through rings, as you can see in this photograph of a jumping pony – the martingale prevents the pony from suddenly throwing back his head; it must be long enough for the reins to form a straight line when the head is held in the normal position. The reins should have leather stops to prevent the martingale rings from catching behind the buckles of the strap ends of the bit.

All this tack must be cleaned regularly if you want to enjoy it for a long time and avoid accidents; when cleaning always check everything for wear and splitting. Keep the saddle clean by removing the sweat and dirt with a damp sponge. Rub a little saddle soap into all leather parts with a damp sponge, after you have removed the stirrup leathers and various buckles, and after taking all the strap ends out of their keepers on the bridle. Wash down the stirrup irons and the bit, and dry them well. Clean the buckles with a dry cloth. Always check that the stitching is not worn and the leather is not split. Rub leather grease or leather oil into the leather parts from time to time, after you have cleaned them and they are dry. But do not do this too often, or the stitching will rot. Then clean the buckles and bit with Brasso, and rinse and dry them. Never use hot water on leather nor hang leather parts in front of a fire to dry. When everything is beautifully clean, hang it all up neatly in the saddle room – the saddle with the stirrup irons run up and the girth hanging loose behind on the saddle horse. The bridle should be hung up neatly on a hook, with the reins taken up through the throat latch and all strap ends through the keepers.

Saddling and unsaddling

Before saddling the pony, fasten him with a halter (you should now know how to do this) and give him a good grooming. There must be no dirt or sweat on him. If there is a gall or sore where the saddle is going to rest, do not saddle him, and certainly do not ride him.

Place the saddle gently on the pony's back, not with a bump or he will take fright. Stand on the pony's left side. The girth should be lying on the saddle and the stirrup irons still run up. Place the saddle a little too far forward at first and then push it gently backwards into position, so that the hairs lie flat.
Pull the numnah up a little into the gullet of the saddle; this is to prevent

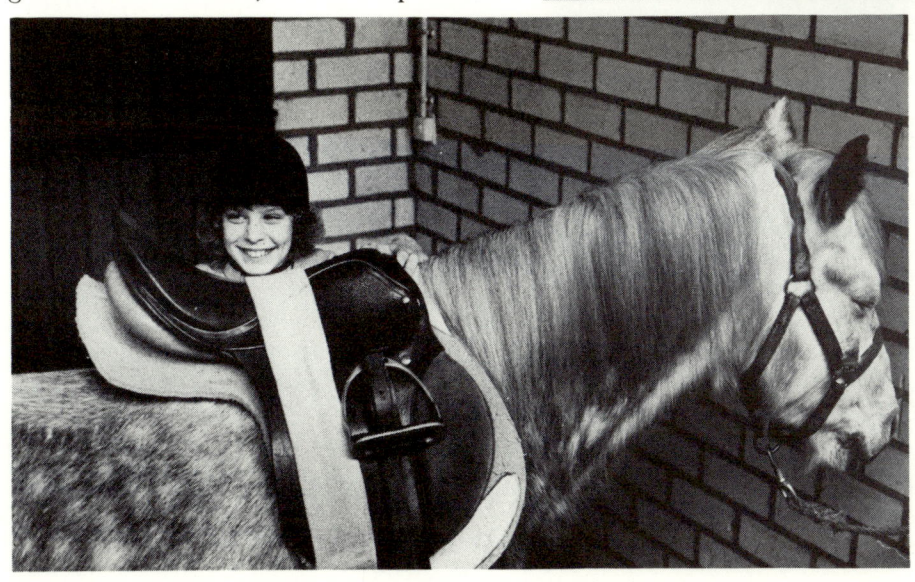

47

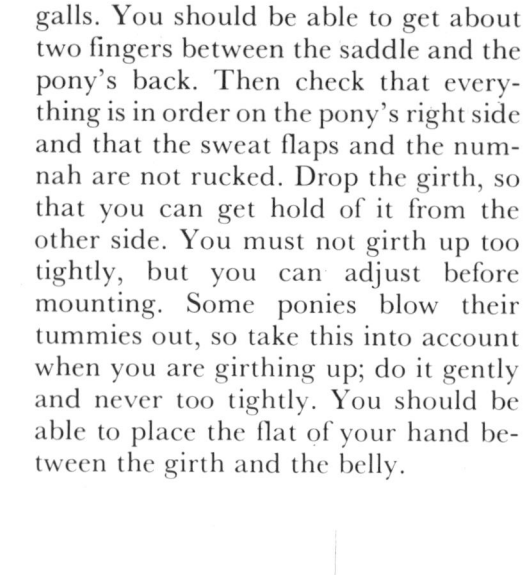

galls. You should be able to get about two fingers between the saddle and the pony's back. Then check that everything is in order on the pony's right side and that the sweat flaps and the numnah are not rucked. Drop the girth, so that you can get hold of it from the other side. You must not girth up too tightly, but you can adjust before mounting. Some ponies blow their tummies out, so take this into account when you are girthing up; do it gently and never too tightly. You should be able to place the flat of your hand between the girth and the belly.

The strap ends and buckles of the girth are underneath the sweat flap of the saddle. In general, we use the outermost strap ends to girth up, while the middle one is a spare. If you fasten the first and second strap ends, the saddle will lie further forward; if you fasten the second and third strap ends, it will lie further back. When breaking in a new saddle, use the first two strap ends, to prevent the saddle from slanting back.

For some ponies, such as Iceland ponies, you will need a tail strap. Do not tighten it until the crupper loop has been fixed under the tail and the saddle is girthed up.

The unsaddling process must be performed with as much care as when you saddled the pony, but it should be done in the reverse order.
Run up the stirrup irons again and lay the girth carefully over the seat of the saddle. Now carefully remove the saddle from the pony's back. Do this before removing the bridle, for the pony likes to roll on the ground after work, and that is bad for the saddle. Besides, without a bridle, the pony might run away with the saddle still on his back.

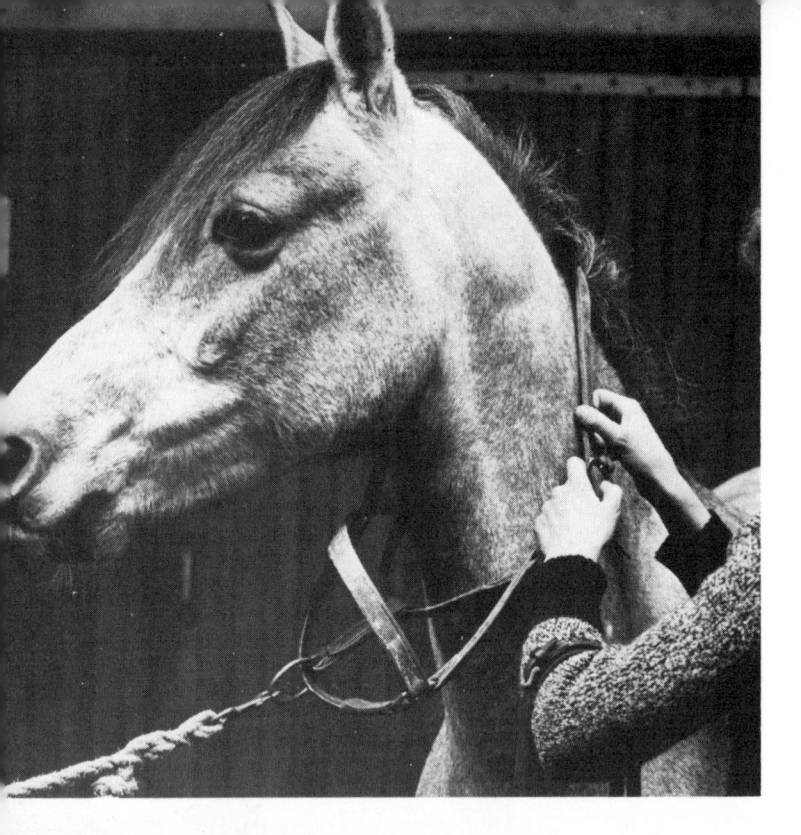

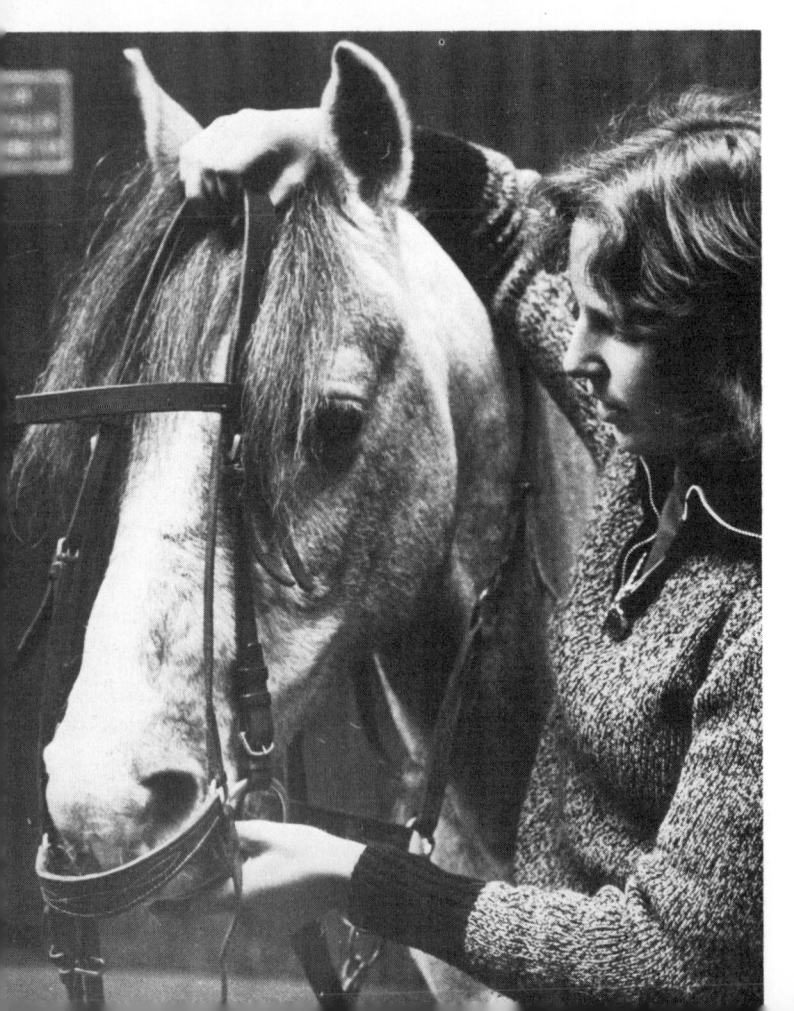

The easiest way of putting a bridle on your pony is to put the halter round his neck. Always work on the near-side of the pony.

Hang the bridle and the reins over your left arm. You can see in the photograph that the horsewoman has the bridle hanging over her hand; the disadvantage of this is that her left hand is not free. Slip the reins over the pony and take hold of the bridle head with your right hand, keeping the snaffle in your left hand. Always put the pony at ease by remaining calm yourself and talking to him.

Push the bit gently against his mouth and bring up the bridle with your right hand. When the pony opens his mouth, push the bit gently into it and place the ears and forelock between the browband and bridle head. If the pony refuses to open his mouth immediately, press with your thumb and forefinger against the 'bars'; in this way you press the lower jaw down, so that you can place the bit in his mouth. If this still does not work, try a lump of sugar. Place the bit in the pony's mouth as soon as he opens it to eat the sugar.

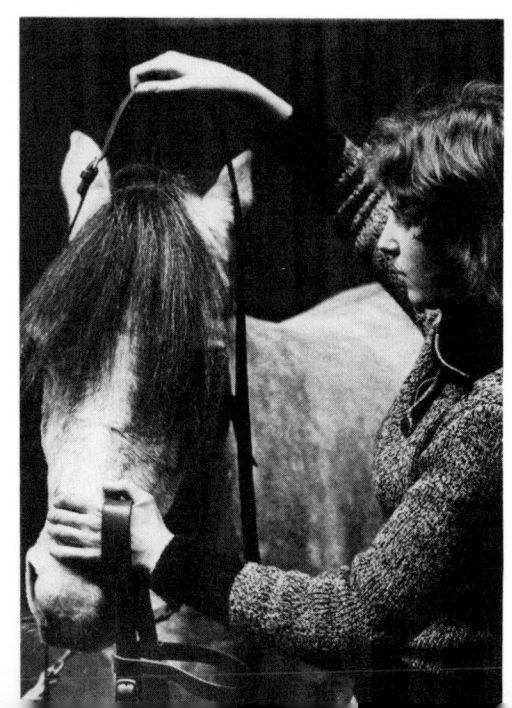

Now pull the forelock out from underneath the browband and make sure that the mane hairs lie flat under the bridle.

The throat latch should be fastened so that you can get your fist between the jaw and the throat latch. The browband must not be too tight either, for the bridle head must not press on the ears. The snaffle rests against the corners of the mouth, without pulling them upwards.

The noseband – whether cavesson or dropped – must sit loosely enough for you to get two fingers underneath it. The dropped noseband lies well above the nostrils and is fastened under the snaffle. If you have a cavesson noseband, it must lie two finger breadths below the end of the cheekbone, under the cheekpieces and over the snaffle.

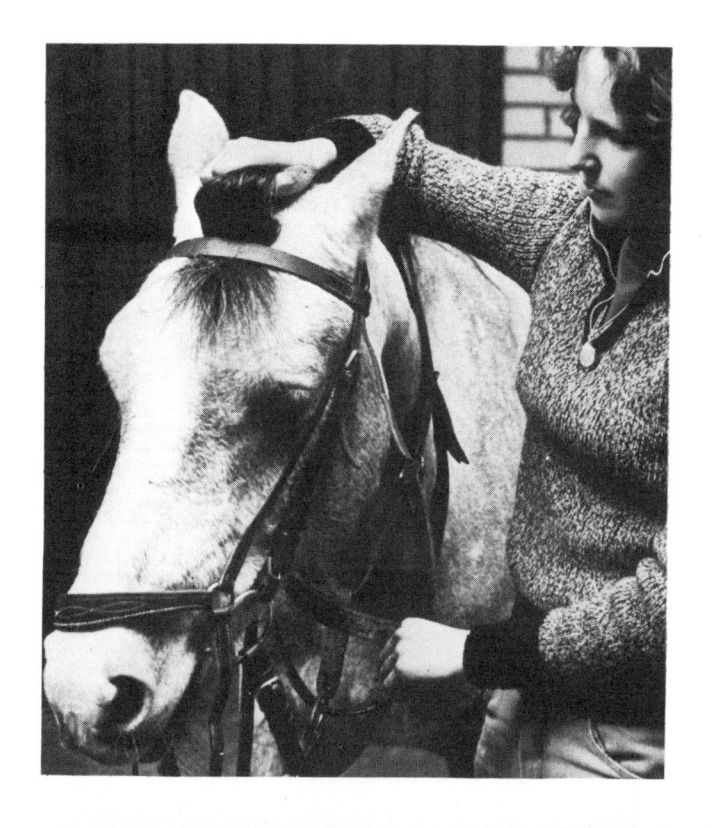

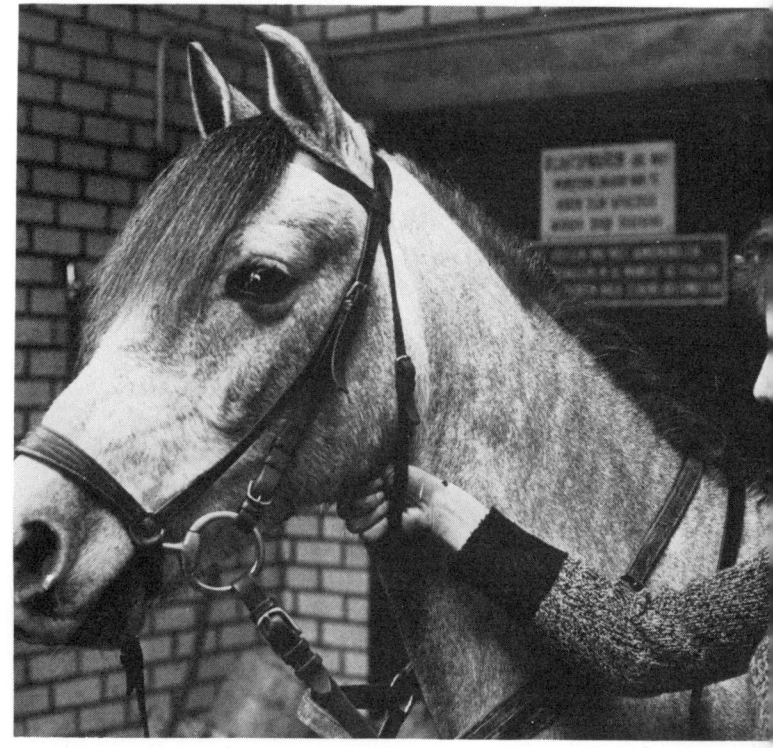

In the photograph you can see a properly bridled and well-groomed pony. All loose strap ends are through the keepers! The mane is plaited here in 'knots'.

When removing the bridle, proceed in the reverse order. Unfasten the throat latch and then the noseband. Lay the reins over the bridle head, take hold of both together and remove the bridle carefully. Catch the bit so that it does not bang the pony's teeth as you take it out of his mouth.

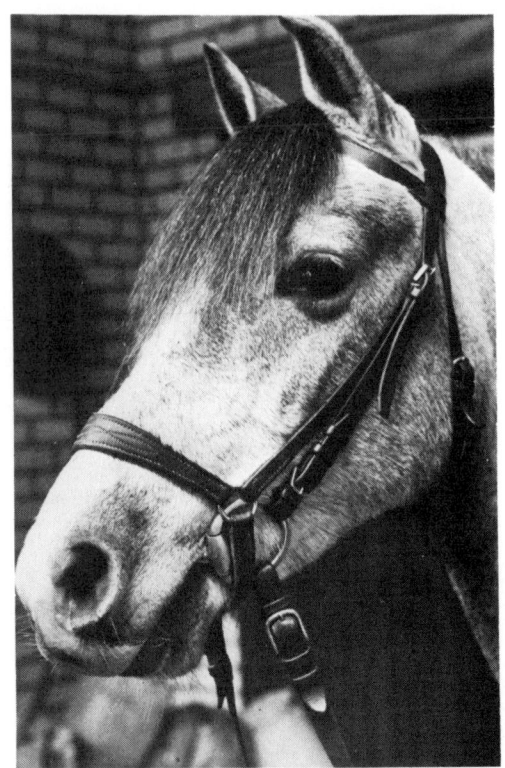

You can see in the photograph how you should carry the saddle and bridle. Nothing should trail on the ground.

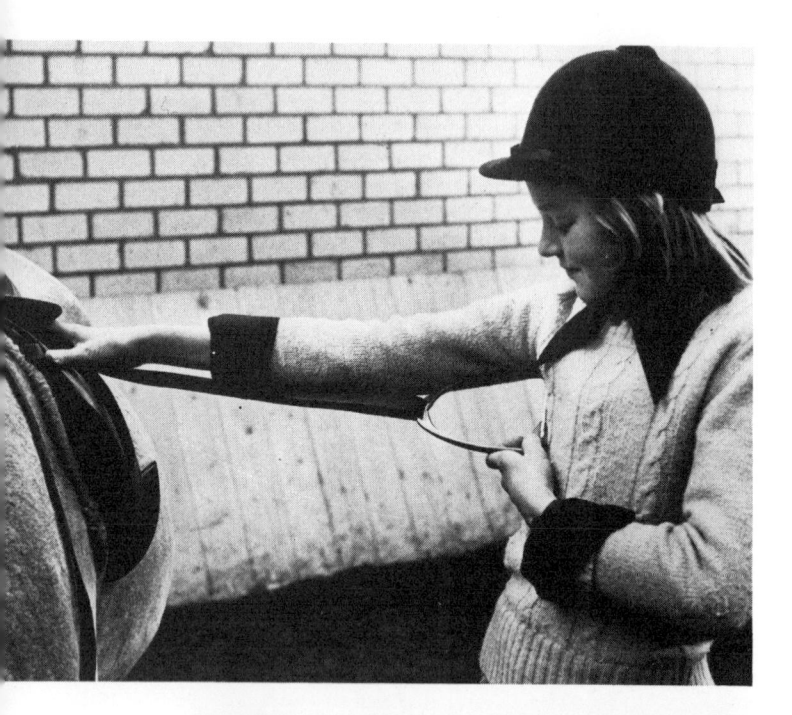

Mounting

Before getting on to the pony, it is important that everything is prepared for mounting. Make sure that the pony is standing four-square (both fore and hind feet beside each other), check the girth and take up the buckles to such an extent that you can still get the flat of your hand underneath. Then let down the two stirrup irons and check that the stirrups are of the right length; do this by placing the finger-tips of your right hand on the buckle and, with your left hand, taking the stirrup leather along your outstretched right arm. The sole of the stirrup iron must reach into your armpit. Keep pulling the stirrup buckle upwards until it comes against the stirrup bar.

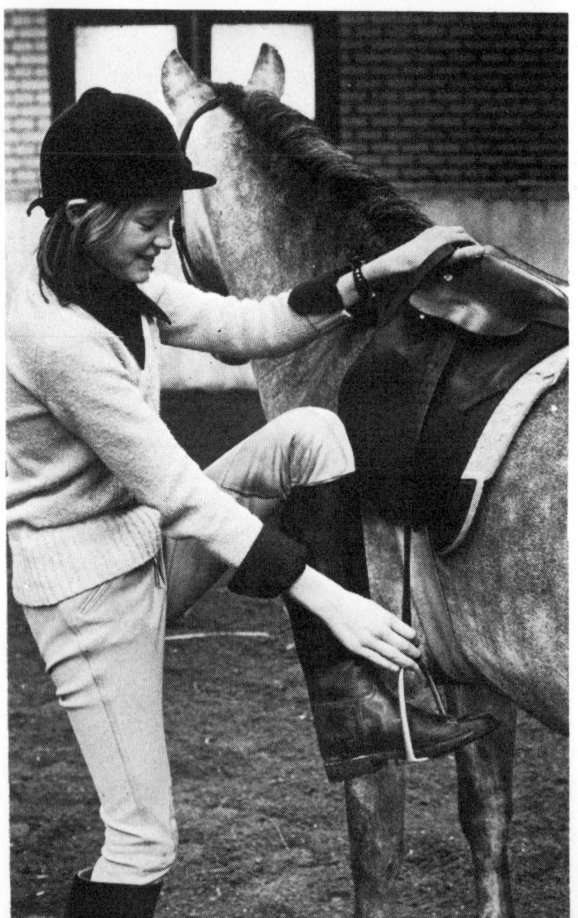

Now you can mount. Stand beside the pony's left shoulder and take the reins in your left hand near the withers, without pulling on them, throwing the slack over the off-side of the pony with your right hand. Stand with your left shoulder close to the pony's left shoulder and, using your right hand, place your left foot in the stirrup iron, turning your foot inwards – but avoid prodding the pony's flank with your toe!

Take three hops forward on your right foot until your chest is turned towards the pony. Grasp the saddle with your left hand just behind the sweat flap. It is better not to hold on to the cantle, or you will pull everything askew. On the third hop, push yourself up from the ground and stretch your left leg. With your left hand, support yourself on the withers and move your right hand on to the pommel.

Then swing your outstretched right leg over the pony's croup, without touching him. Place your right knee against the sweat flap of the saddle and sit down gently, turning your right foot into the stirrup iron.

Finally, take the reins in both hands. They should run from the pony's mouth between your little finger and ring finger, across the palm of your hand and out between your thumb and index finger. Your thumbs resting on the reins should be bent. The end of the reins should rest against the right-hand side of the pony's neck.

It may be that the stirrups do not hang evenly. You can see this by standing in front of the pony. Since we always mount on the near-side, the left stirrup leather will stretch more; so check the stirrup leathers regularly for this (and wear) and, if necessary, change round the left and right stirrup leathers.
If the stirrups are even and of the right length, you can move off.

Dismounting

Having dealt with mounting, we must now consider how to dismount. For dismounting, you do exactly the same things as for mounting, but in reverse order.

First of all take both reins in your left hand and place your right hand forward in the saddle near the pommel. Lay your left hand, which is holding the reins, on the pony's withers.

Take your right foot out of the stirrup iron and stretch your left leg. Then swing your right leg out in one movement over the pony's croup, without touching him.

Let go of the reins with your left hand and push your left arm between the reins. The left stirrup iron is now pushed up along the rear leather and the end of the leather is pushed through the iron. Now loosen the two buckles of the girth a few holes, walk across in front of the pony and push your right hand between the reins, then run up the right stirrup iron. Walk back across in front of the pony, take the reins over the pony's head and lead him to the stable.

Good posture and seat

Before you learn to have a good seat, you must know what the initial posture should be: your legs should hang loosely down against the pony, with the flat side of your thigh bone and knee against the saddle. If you can imagine a perpendicular line dropped from your knee to the ground, then the toe of your foot should touch that line. The ball of your foot should be on the stirrup iron, while the heel should be the lowest point. Your trunk and head should be held erect, but not too stiffly. You should be able to feel the collar of your jacket against your neck. Look straight ahead, keeping your shoulders back and down. Let your arms hang naturally at your sides, with the elbows close to your body. The forearms should point in the direction of the pony's mouth, with the wrists turned slightly outwards and the hands with the thumb uppermost.

The most important part of a good seat is balance and the 'independence' of the seat: keep your weight equally distributed, so that you sit comfortably and do not restrict the pony's movements. First, sit with both seat bones in the deepest part of the saddle, with the flat inside of your thighs against the saddle. The deepest part of the saddle must be over the deepest part of the pony's back. This is the least mobile and the strongest part of the pony's back, and this is also where it is easiest for riders to follow the pony's movements; it is just behind the withers.

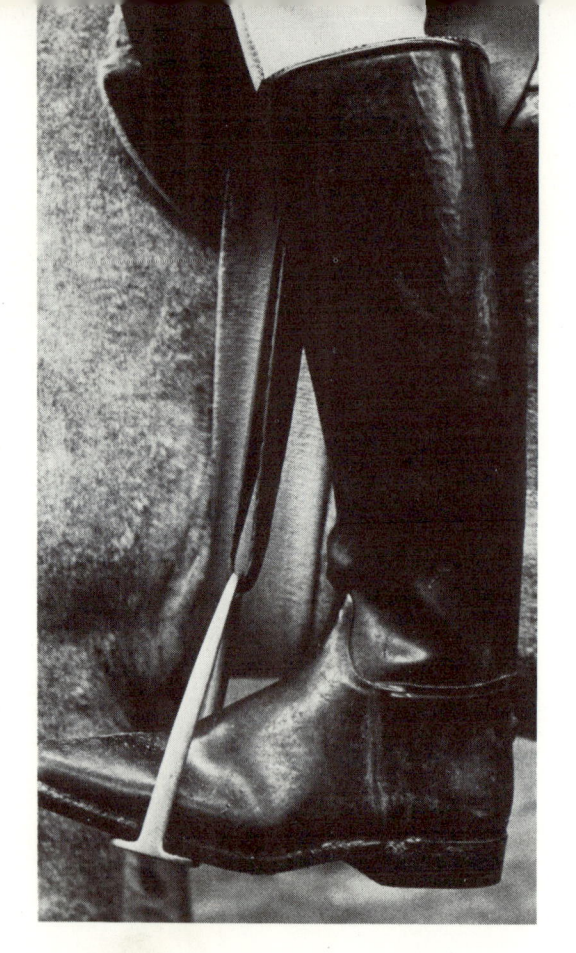

The broadest part of your foot (the ball of the foot) should be supported in the stirrup iron. The heel should be a little lower than the toe, but do not overdo this. The ankles must be flexible to absorb some of the shocks during riding. Your calf – or the inside of your boot – should rest against the pony and should always keep good contact with him. No part of you must be stiff, especially your knees; you should let your knees give way, so that your lower leg falls naturally against the pony.

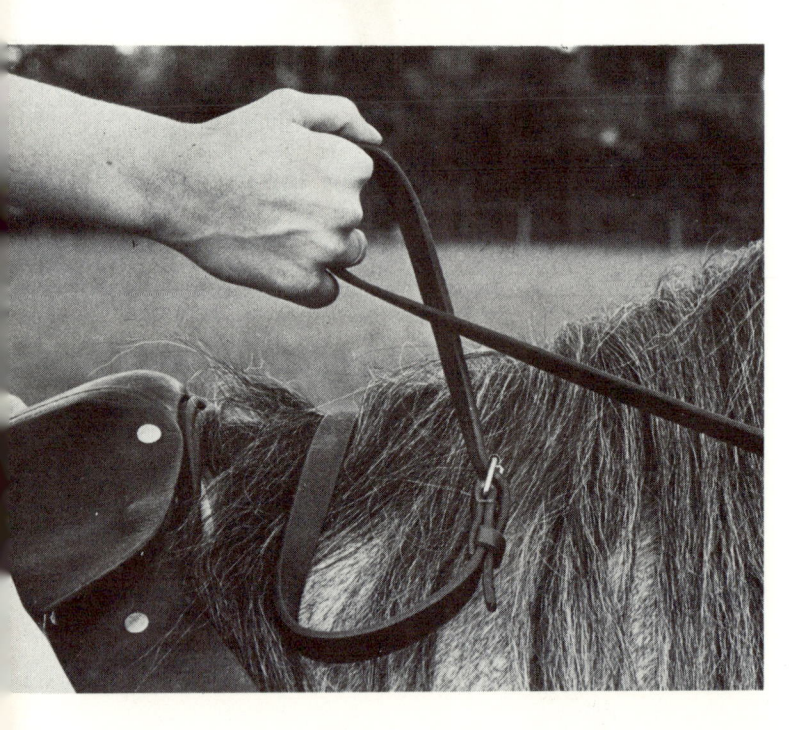

Let your hands and arms hang naturally from your shoulders, so that the elbows are loose and your fingers and wrists are supple. Your elbows should be just in front of your hips, never behind them! The forearm should be in line with the rein and will form a straight line from the elbow to the bit. Keep both hands at the same height, one on each side of the neck, just above the gullet of the saddle. The thumbs should be on top, and the knuckles should point forward. Your wrists must be supple to enable you to follow all the movements of your pony's mouth. Good hands are those which consistently 'give' with the pony's mouth, so that the reins are kept slightly taut.

Sit up straight, but not stiffly, for you must be in unison with all the pony's movements. Look straight ahead, with your head erect and your shoulders held back and down. An imaginary line drawn from your shoulders through your hips to your heel would be straight.

In order to learn all this well, it is best to begin with sitting exercises on the lunge. Hold on to the pommel at first for it is better to begin properly than to unlearn faults later.

Then let go of the saddle and try to do some simple exercises, such as arms at your sides, feet out of the stirrup irons, and so forth.

If all that goes well, you can take the reins and try to keep light contact with the pony's mouth.

Riding without stirrups is a good way of learning to acquire a good seat. Do make sure that you let your legs hang naturally, with the heels low, and that you do not pinch the pony with your knees and thighs. This could have the wrong effect on the pony, and you could acquire bad habits. Similarly, if you persevere too long and become tired, you may take up the wrong position.

If you are riding with your feet out of the stirrups, you should cross the stirrups over in front of the saddle. Do the same thing when doing exercises on the pony.

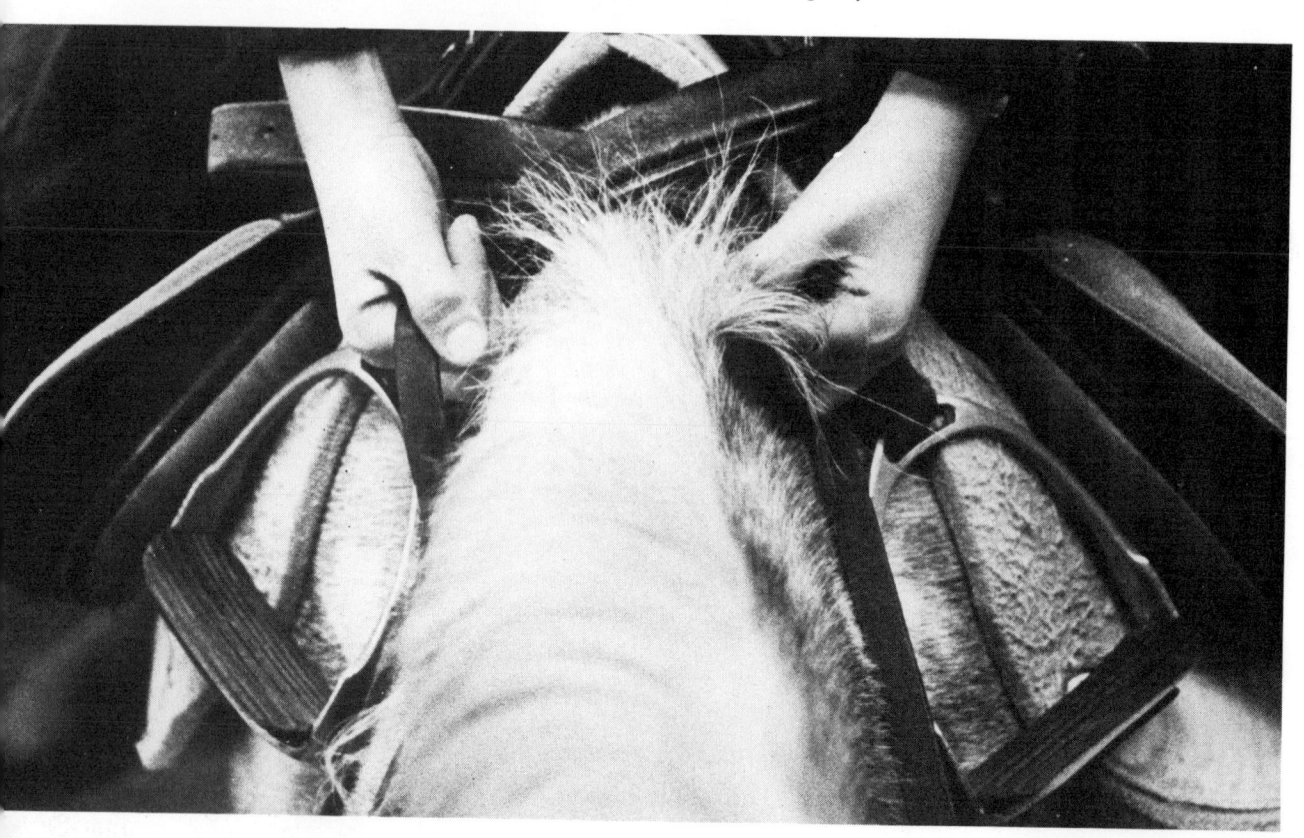

We shall come back to exercises in later chapters, but they are very important for giving you an 'independent' seat. An independent seat means that you control certain parts of your body, individually, without reflexes. A reflex is an unconscious movement which you make without thinking about it. For example, if you look right, your lower left leg moves forward automatically. The idea is that you should be able to move all parts of your body independently. You can use the riding aids efficiently only if your knee rests firmly against the saddle and you are able to control the movements of your lower leg. Practice is therefore important.

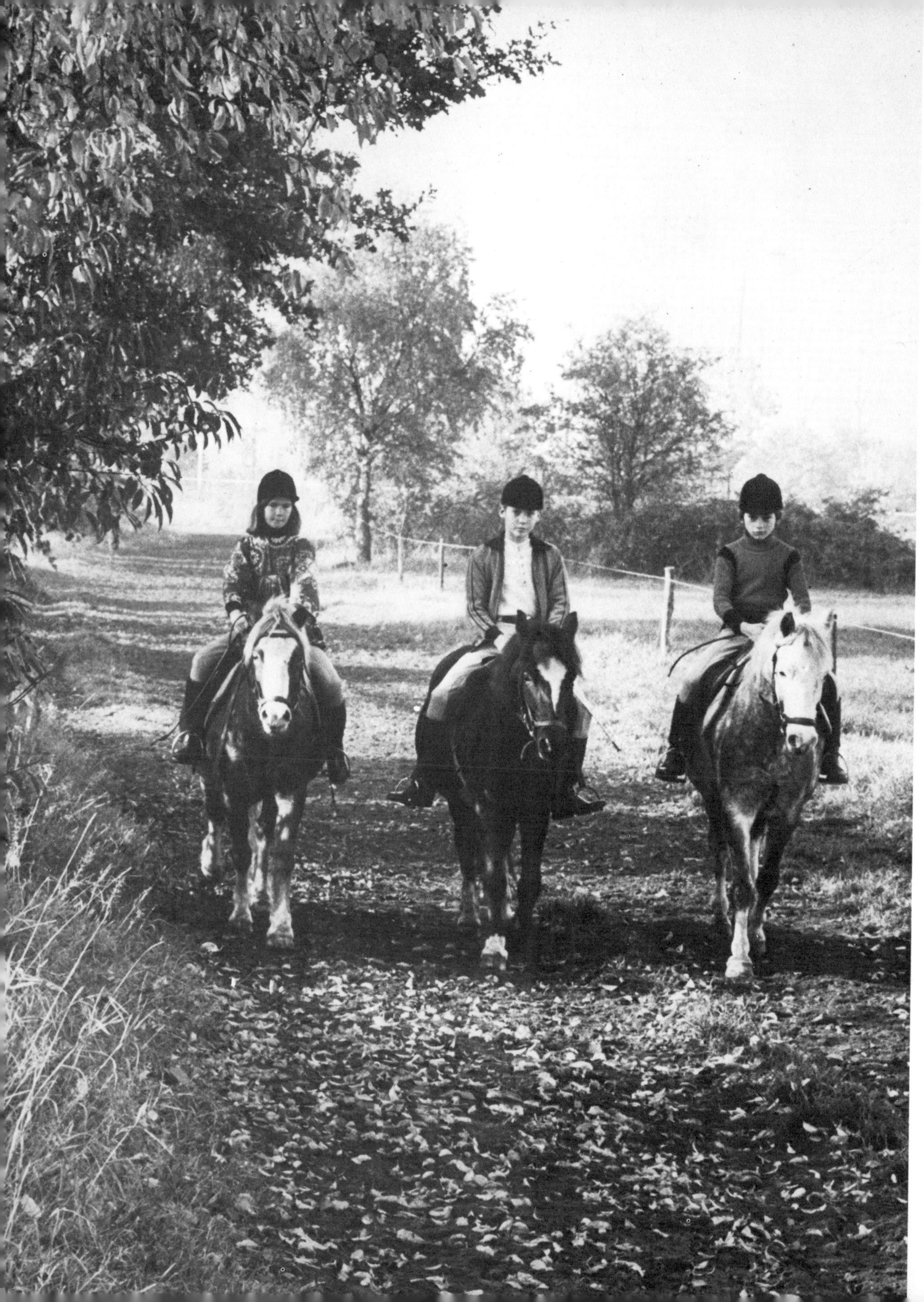

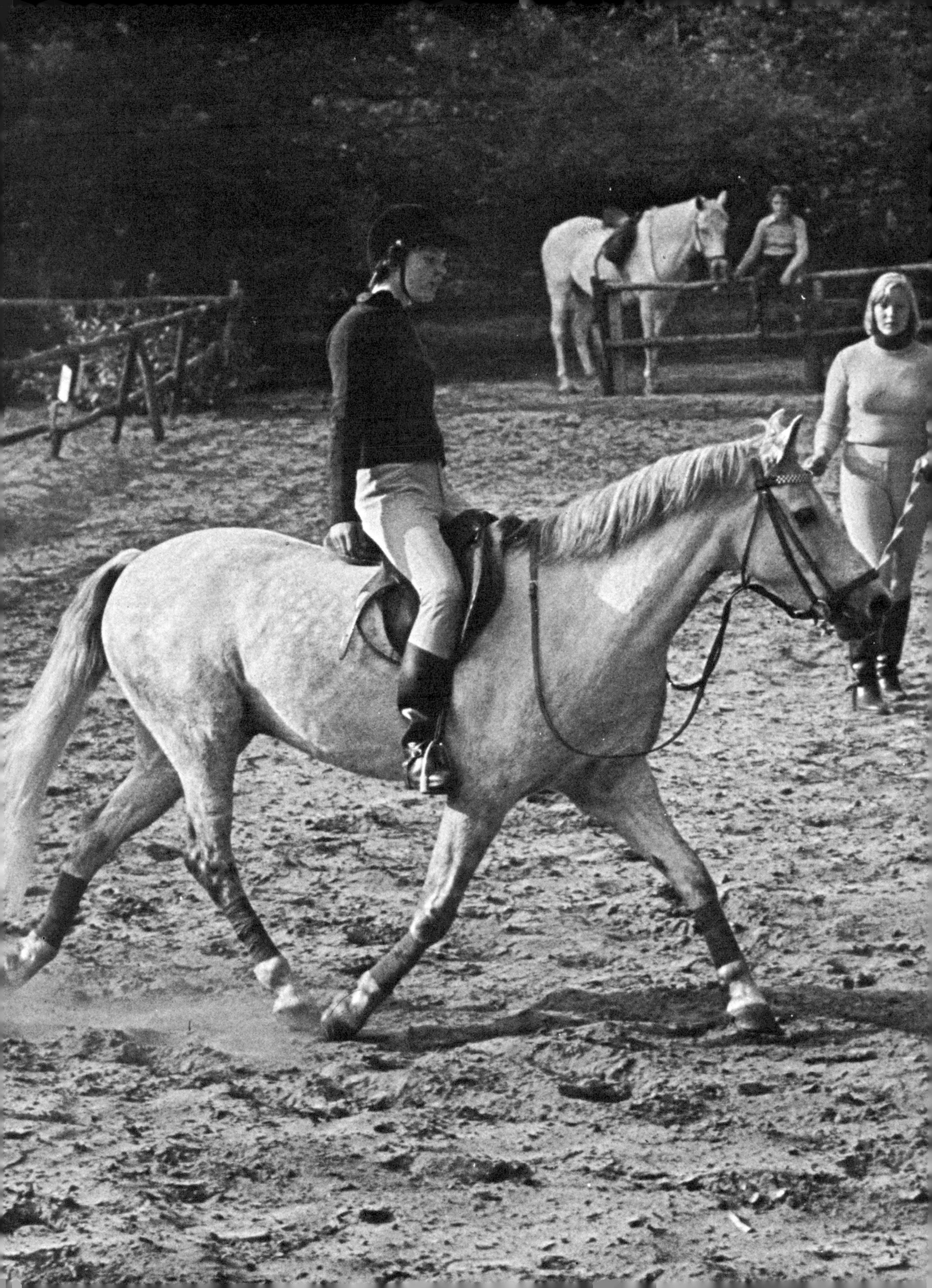

How the pony moves

In the previous chapters we practised mounting and dismounting and studied the seat; now it is time for us to start riding. In the illustration you can see the correct seat; the horsewoman is sitting erect, her legs are positioned properly and her forearm forms a straight line with the reins.

Horses and ponies move in three ways, called the three gaits: the *walk*, the *trot* and the *canter*. There are other gaits, like the *'rack'* and the ambling gait of Iceland ponies, but they are exceptions, and we shall leave them out. It is very important in all the gaits that you should 'follow' your pony's mouth well with your hand. In the photograph, you can see how the rider walking her pony keeps 'contact' with the pony's mouth, with the rein slightly flexed. In the walk, your hand must flex and respond to the movement of the mouth.

Changing gait or pace is called a 'transition'; so if you want to go from a walk to a trot, you make a transition. Give the pony a squeeze with both calves just behind the girth, without raising your heels, and open your hands to allow the pony to go forward. At each transition you must, as it were, 'sit deeper into the saddle'; this means that you move forward from the lower back, your sitting bones go forward and you get a somewhat hollow lower back. Remember that all aids must work together in a transition. Above all, you must never pull on the reins, not even in the transition from trot to walk.

Can you see in this photograph that the pony is trotting? Just compare this photograph with the previous one, in which the pony is walking. The sequence in which the pony puts his legs down is different in each of the gaits: in technical terms, the walk is a four-time movement, the trot is a two-time movement and a canter is a three-time movement.

If you take your pony out on a hard road, you will be able to distinguish these clearly. In the walk you hear four hoofbeats with equal pauses; the four feet make contact with the ground in turn. In the trot you hear two hoofbeats, for in this case the pony always puts two feet to the ground simultaneously, with what is known as the diagonal pairs of feet. In other words: off-fore and near-hind together, or near-fore and off-hind together. Between each of the hoofbeats the pony is suspended just for a moment above the ground: this is known as the period of suspension. In the canter you hear three hoofbeats – first from one of the hind legs (eg, near-hind), then from a diagonal pair of legs (eg, off-hind and near-fore), and finally, from the fourth leg (eg, off-fore). After this there is a period of suspension. The canter is a sort of leaping gait.

Can you see from the photograph that the pony here is in a canter? The pony must first be very well trained in the walk and trot to be able to strike off easily into a canter.

There are two possibilities in the canter, right or left. The pony in the photograph is cantering on the right rein: this means that he always places his off-fore and his off-hind in front of his near-fore and hind legs – you can see that his inside foreleg, here his off-leg, always reaches further forward. If you are turning to the right, you must canter on the right rein, and if you are turning to the left, you canter on the left rein.

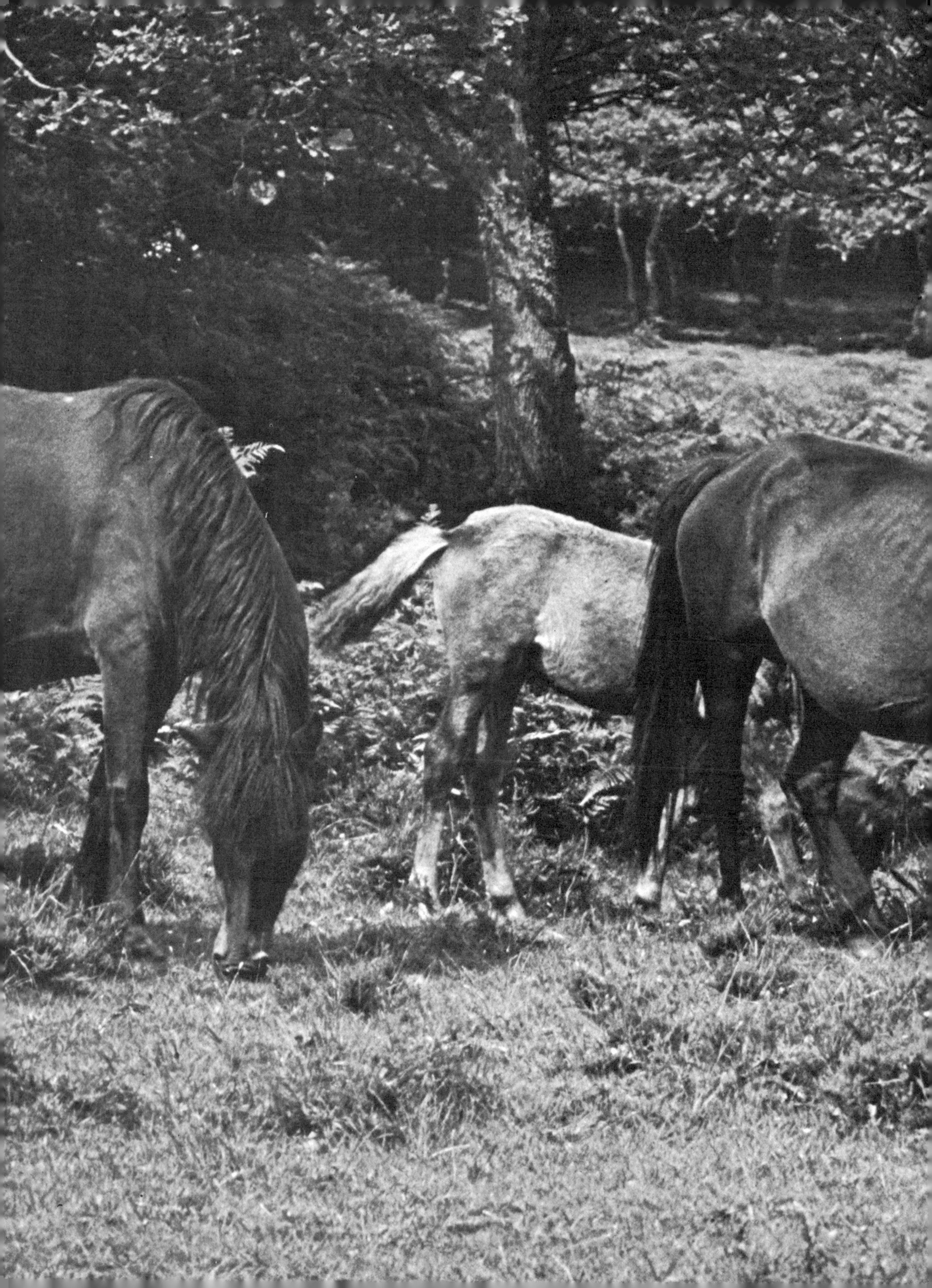

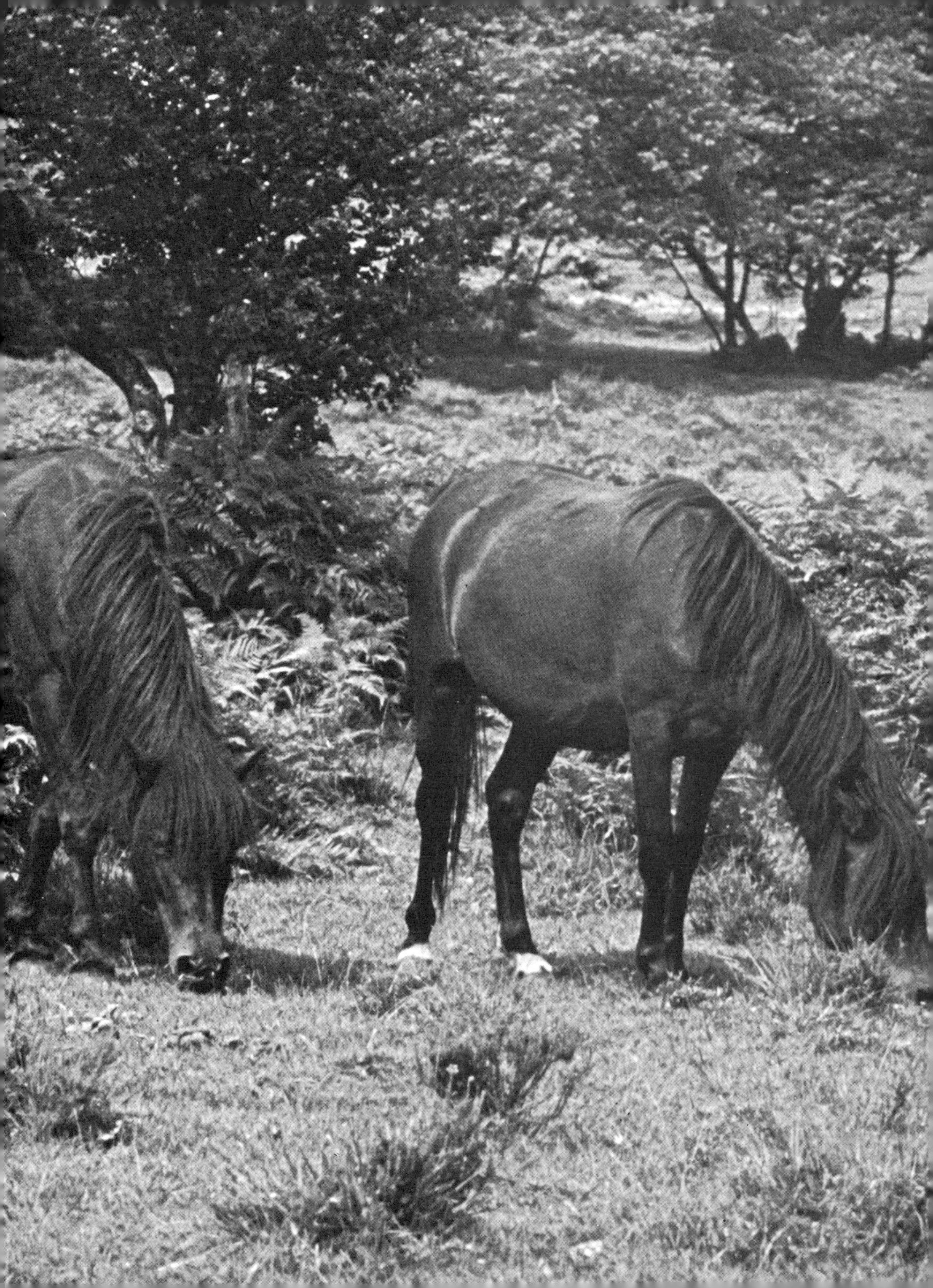

Sitting and rising trot

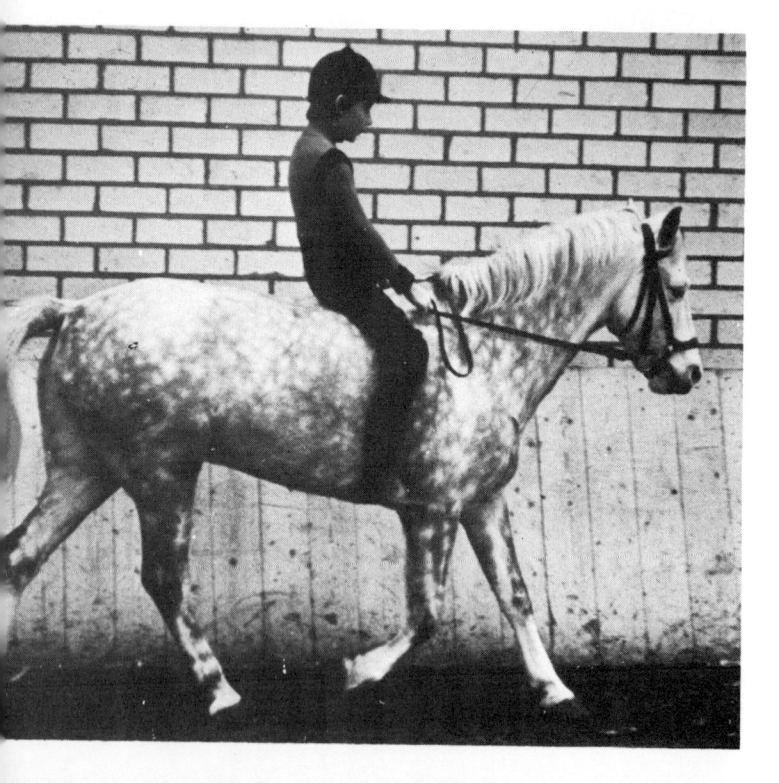

It is very important that you keep the correct posture when you go slower or faster; keep your balance and do not sit rigidly or stiffly, but stretch your body. When you think that you can stay relaxed and in the right position, take a look at the shoulder and shoulder joint movements of the pony in the trot. The movements of the pony's back are much greater in the trot than in the walk. It now becomes more difficult to remain seated well. In the trot you can sit in two ways, ie, sitting or rising.

The sitting trot

In the sitting trot you remain seated in the saddle and try to move with the pony's back, although you are thrown upwards by it each time. It is used mainly for schooling, when doing figures and turns. You get a good feel of the pony if you sit on its bare back and then do the trot. It is not easy at the beginning to maintain a full seat. Because you often hold your lower back too stiffly at the beginning, you jar and bump at every step of the trot. You must frequently practise the trot without stirrups in order to learn to maintain the full seat. In this case you cross the stirrups in front of the saddle. Make sure that your lower back is quite supple and that you follow closely the movements of the pony's back. Do not become tense or cling with your knees. Stretch your body and let yourself sink into the saddle.

The off foreleg and the near-hind leg are on the ground. If you are riding the rising trot on the right diagonal, you should now be sitting in the saddle.

The rising trot

You will be able to understand this more easily if you look again at the positioning of the pony's legs as described earlier. We saw that the pony lifts and puts down his legs diagonally in the trot. You also know that the trot has a moment of suspension. If the pony puts down his off-fore and near-hind legs together, we say that he is on the right diagonal – so named from the foreleg of the diagonal in question. In the rising trot (which is also called the posting trot), your seat should go up and down in time with one of the two diagonal pairs of legs. When the pony puts down his near foreleg, which is the left diagonal, and when you are sitting in the saddle, then you are riding on the left diagonal.

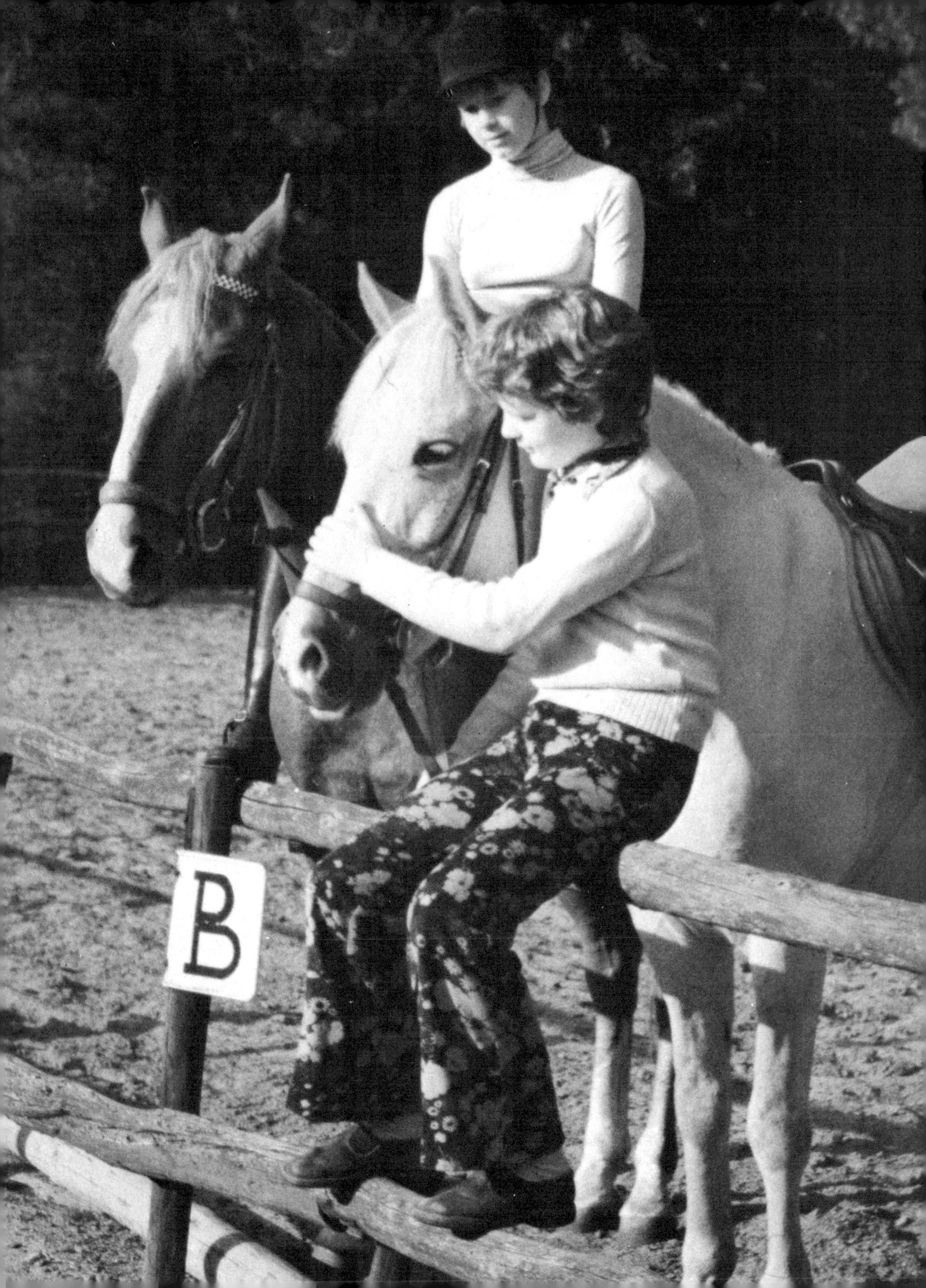
B

The near foreleg and the off-hind leg are on the ground. If you are riding the rising trot on the right diagonal, you should now be rising from the saddle.

You come out of the saddle, therefore, as the pony's near foreleg leaves the ground; you let yourself be thrown up by your pony and you brace yourself with your knees and on your stirrups. Do not stand in the stirrups.

So if you sit in the saddle when the pony puts down his off foreleg and come out of the saddle when he lifts his off foreleg, you are riding on the right diagonal.

In the *manège*, the enclosure where you are taught to ride, you always sit on the outside foreleg, in other words, on the outside diagonal. This is called sitting on the correct leg. You come out of the saddle as little as possible. The upper part of your body may go forward a little, but you must not stick out your bottom. Your lower legs should stay in place, with your heels low. You must not push off from your stirrups, but allow yourself to be pushed up by your pony's back. The reins are not there for you to pull on. Your hands should remain still, independent of the rest of your body. In a good rising trot, you should ride with your seat well forwards.

You should use this method of trotting in the *manège*, but it is also useful when out riding in the woods.

The aids: learning to talk to your pony

We now come to a more difficult chapter: on the aids to riding. What are these aids? Aids are signals which have been thought out logically, bearing in mind the pony's nature. The pony is taught these signals; he must be able to distinguish between them, and the rider must use them correctly, if they are to understand each other. So they are a sort of language used between rider and pony.

First of all, there are the leg aids. Your calves have an important part to play in producing and maintaining impulsion (forward movement). Impulsion is essential if you are to control your pony well. If you want to go forwards, you press both calves lightly against the pony just behind the girth, in the rhythm of his movement, and yield a little with your hands.

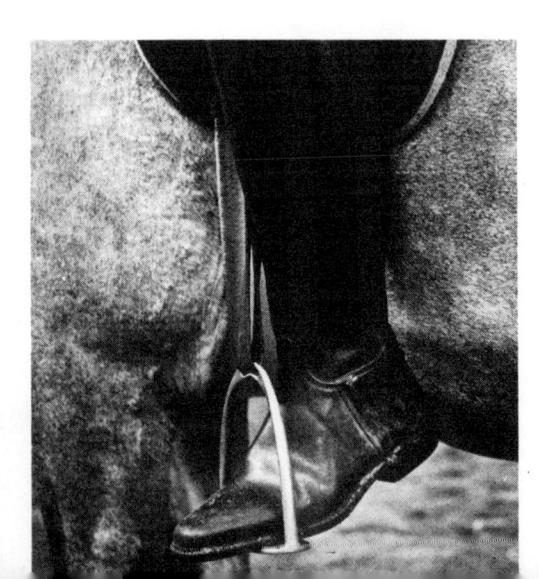

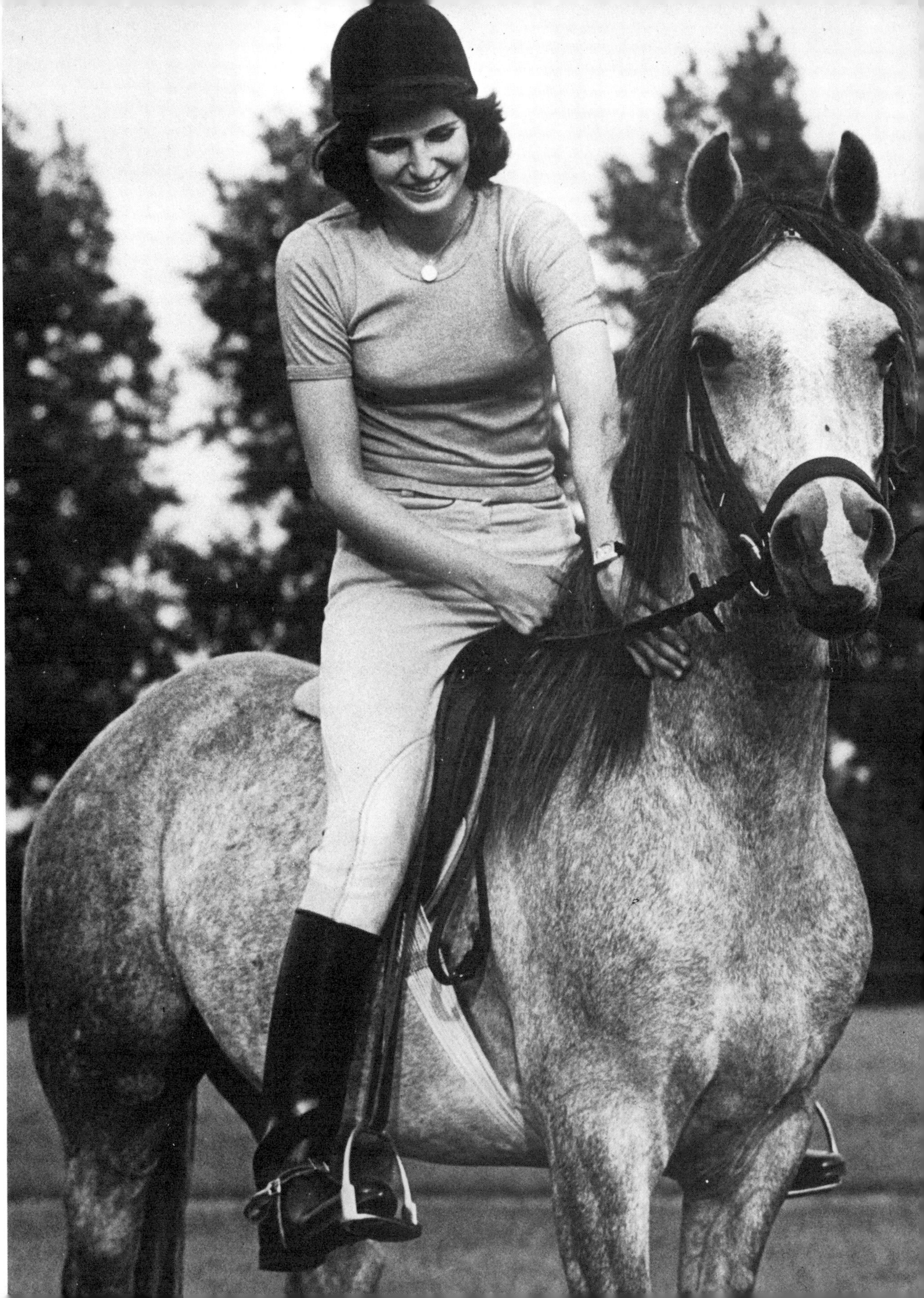

It is not necessary to raise your heels, as in the photograph. Your calves should remain where they are, and you should repeat the aid, a little more firmly if necessary. So your heels should stay low and your knees remain in contact – not as in the photograph, where the rider's knees are out of contact with the pony. It is also wrong to keep jerking your legs or your heels. In the end the pony will not react and the aid will fail.

To teach your pony to move more readily with pressure from the calf, you can use a stick (riding whip). Give your pony a tap on the shoulder as you press with your calves. When you are riding a little better, use a slightly longer whip and, as you press with your calves, tap with it just behind the calf, and you will see that the pony is very quick to obey a gentle instruction. You must stop using these or other aids as soon as the pony obeys. In addition to the whip, you can use your voice as well, by saying, for example, "Forward", simultaneously with the other driving aids. You can also use your voice when you want to slow down or halt, by saying "Whoa."

At dressage competitions you must not use your voice. There is nothing wrong with rewarding your pony with a pat on the neck and a friendly word. He will then be sure that you understand each other.

Apart from the whip and the voice, there is another aid which can support your leg aids: the spurs. But before you use spurs, you must be able to keep your lower legs still at all times and have complete control over them.

The rider's weight can be a great help in controlling the pony. At the beginning you will not be able to sit so well or so independently, and your weight will be more of a hindrance than a help. You must learn to distribute your weight between your two sitting bones and to follow the pony's movements with your seat. Then you will be able to shift your weight in such a way that it will assist the leg and rein aids. For example, by exerting greater pressure on the left stirrup and stretching your left side, you instruct the pony to turn left, as you can see here. The weight is then on your left sitting bone. You can help yourself by always looking in the direction in which you are going.

If you want to halt, stretch the upper part of your body and sit deeply in the saddle. By shifting your weight in this way, you tell the pony that he must slow down.

The rein conveys to the pony the signals which you give with your hand; it does so by means of the snaffle, which acts on the sensitive 'bars' in the pony's mouth. A good hand is most important and a firm and independent seat is the prime requirement for a good hand. Good hands are mostly passive; they follow the movements of the pony's mouth. This is called a yielding hand: in other words, it yields to the movements of the pony's mouth. If you want to be able to give good rein aids, you must maintain light and supple contact, keeping your elbows, wrists and fingers elastic, like the rider in the photograph.

Your hands offer resistance (hold without pulling) when you want to make a transition to a slower pace or when you want to halt. You must never pull. It is therefore necessary for you to be able to sit so independently that you are able to offer resistance without pulling, and without your lower legs going forward. You must never offer resistance before pressing with your legs. If you want to ride your pony up into the bridle, you must squeeze more with your calves, then immediately resist, and then relax your hands again quickly. The rider here is pulling, and the pony is resisting the rein. So you must learn right from the start never to contradict the riding aids with your hands. The resistance of the hands must never be greater than the resistance of the pony, and you must relax your hands immediately the pony stops resisting.

As we said before, the aids must never contradict one another. Here we see a yielding rein aid. If you want to go forward, you urge the pony forward and your hands then yield, so that the pony can actually go forward.

All aids must be given to the right degree – not too much and not too little. Here, too much resistance is being given, while the calves are not creating enough forward impulsion. As a result the pony is moving behind the bit.

Your hands should be held one on each side of the crest. Nor should they be crossed over it, or the pony could then break away over the shoulder, which has much the same effect as a car going into a skid. The hands control forward movement by means of the reins. This impulsion is produced by the calves. So you ride the pony, as it were, up into the bit.

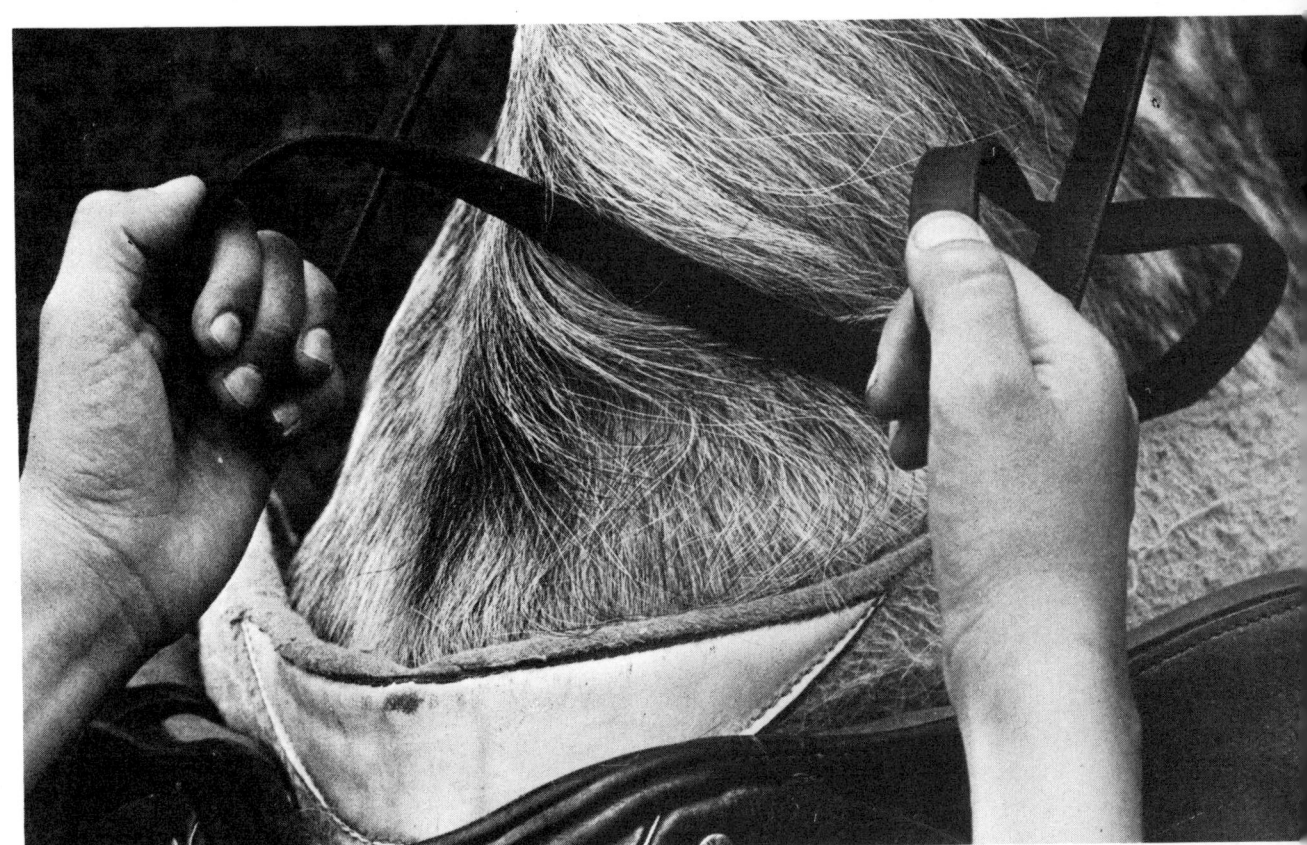

In order to make a transition to halt, you should ride your pony with seat and calves towards the transition, while your hands offer resistance. Stretch out the upper part of your body and slide your sitting bones forward in the saddle, so that your lower back is somewhat arched. In this way the pony is ridden up into the hand, and the hands reduce their yielding movements and finally remain still. The pony now stands still without resistance, having brought his quarters underneath his body. We can see clearly here how all aids must work together – first the impelling aids of seat and calves, and only then the rein aids.

Here we see the riding of a turn to the right. You give weight aids for a right turn by putting your weight on your right seat bone and pressing down your right heel. You should remain with your seat and calves driving forward, while your right hand should move a little forward and to the right, and your left hand also moves to the right and forward. The left rein gives as much as the right wants. Always look where you are going, and your pony, too, must always look where he is going.

The inside leg (R) in the lower illustration should be on the girth, the outside leg (2) should be just behind the girth.

At pony games and gymkhanas you will find that if you lean towards a particular side, the pony will automatically turn that way, unless you give counteracting aids. The pony in this photograph will go easily to the right, but not so easily to the left. You can see why for yourself.

Let us now just repeat briefly how good aids are given. First of all, they must be properly combined and given smoothly. They must be used almost invisibly and to the right extent, and the point at which you give the particular aids must be right – in other words, not too early and not too late. In this photograph the rider has her calves close to the pony and can therefore give the correct leg aids in the right place at the right time. Her hand is also in the right place and it will be able to coordinate with the legs.

If you are making the transition from trot to canter, you must give the aids as follows.

You should produce more impulsion with both calves and your reins should be fairly taut. Now move both hands out a little, maintaining equally taut reins, and shift your weight on to your inside seat bone by stretching on the inside. Your outside calf should be back a little and your inside calf should be on the girth. You then take off into the canter by squeezing with your calves and yielding with your hands. You can do this best in a corner of the *manège* or in a volt, that is, a circle traced by the horse's movements. Your outside calf and your inside calf should remain actively in the rhythm of the canter. Your hands should follow the pony's mouth and you should sit upright. If you are not doing very well, ask an experienced instructor to help you, for it is difficult to lose bad habits which you may acquire while doing this – this applies to everything you do!

Exercises in the saddle

In the chapter on posture and seat, we saw that you must be able to sit independently on your pony. Sitting independently means that you have to be able to move your arms, legs and head independently of your trunk and of one another. In order to achieve this, you have to do exercises, and for two reasons: first, it makes a pleasant change and diversion in the riding lesson; second, you will find that your riding is easier and better. It is advisable to do special exercises to cure particular faults.

At the beginning, you should keep your feet in the stirrups, but, if all goes well, you can take your feet out and hang the stirrups crossed in front of the saddle. Make a knot in the reins on the side of the neck so that they hang on the mane. Start by rolling your head: first, right forward, then right back, then from left to right, and, finally, all the way round. Your neck muscles will become relaxed, and you will learn to move your head without your trunk, arms or legs moving as well.

The next exercise is to make backward circles with one arm. Let your arms hang down loosely with your legs still in place. Now make large circles backwards with one arm. Do it slowly at the beginning, then increase your speed. Your other arm should hang still, and your legs must not move. Check that this is so! Then do it with the other arm. This exercise will increase the suppleness of your shoulders – something which is necessary for good hands.

In order to be able to look around you freely and to give the right weight aids, you must practise twisting the upper part of your body to the left and to the right. First, place your hands on your hips. Then twist your trunk round from the waist; your head must turn as well, but your hips should remain still. Turn first to the left, then right round to the right. Try to turn as far to the back as possible.

In this photograph the movement is being done incorrectly: the lower leg is moving forward, instead of staying in place. The rider is leaning back too far, so his back is curved. You must move only the upper part of your body, independently of the lower part.

If you find it difficult to do the sitting trot because you are stiff in the loins (the part below the hips), you must do the following exercise often and, above all, correctly – bending the upper part of your body to the side. Sit erect, with your hands hanging naturally at your sides. Now bend sideways in line with your hips and try to slide your hand as far as possible down your leg. Make sure that you do not lean forwards, but only sideways. Do this to the left, and then to the right.

Now we come to raising the thighs. We start with one thigh, holding on to the pommel of the saddle with one hand. Lift your knee up to the withers and lower it again. The upper part of your body should remain straight and still. When you can keep your balance well, raise both knees towards each other above the withers and place your lower legs against the pony's shoulder blades. Try to hold this position for as long as possible. It will strengthen the muscles of your abdomen and thighs. Make sure that the upper part of your body remains as it was when you started. You must not do any of these exercises too often or for too long, or you run the risk of becoming tired and doing the exercises wrongly.

We are now going to make lifting the thighs more difficult, by bending the upper part of the body forward at the same time and taking the head to the knees. Then go back to the starting position. Your arms should always hang loosely by your sides. This exercise is to give suppleness to the loins, so that you learn to bend and stretch them. This makes it possible to 'stick' in the saddle during the sitting trot, for example.

In the next exercise you put your outside leg over the pony's neck. Take hold of the pommel of the saddle with your inside hand, stretch out your outside leg and swing it over the pony's neck. In doing this, you must not touch the pony. If you find it difficult, you can hold on to the cantle of the saddle initially with your outside hand. The leg which is not swung over stays in position. This is not being done very well in the photograph.

An exercise which helps you to learn good positioning of the knee and thigh bone is rolling the thighs. It brings the inside front part of your thigh and calf against the saddle, instead of the outside back part of the thigh, which would take your knee out of contact. This is how you do it: hold on to the pommel with one hand, lift your thigh sideways, bring it out backwards from your hips and then turn it in the hip joint, so that the inside of your knee points towards the saddle. Then push your knee hard forward along the saddle. When rolling your right thigh, do not – as in the photograph – hold on to the saddle with your left hand, but with your right hand, and when you are rolling your left thigh, hold on with your left hand.

In order to slacken the knee, which you were holding fairly stiffly in the previous exercise, you continue by swinging the left and right lower legs. A loose and supple knee joint is necessary for producing impulsion from the calf, while the knee remains firmly against the saddle. Now let your lower leg swing backwards and forwards away from the pony – so far backwards that you can put your hand round your ankle. The other leg must stay in place.

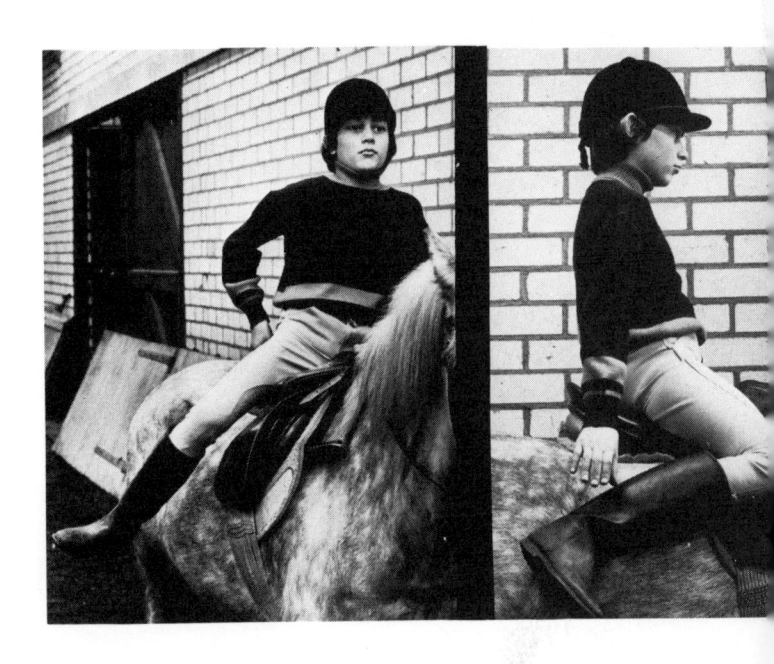

An exercise which will make your ankles supple is circling with the point of your foot. Sit erect and relaxed, with your arms hanging loosely by your sides. Make circular movements to left and right with the point of your foot. Supple knees and ankles help to keep your lower legs in position and you will be able to give better leg aids when the knee and lower leg are in their proper place.

The preceding exercises can be made more difficult by doing them during a slow trot. The photograph shows how to make circles with each arm in turn doing the trot. You can make it more difficult by doing two exercises at once, for example, swinging one arm and rolling your head to look towards the swinging arm, or swinging both arms backwards in turn, etc. You must do all these exercises correctly, and make sure that your seat remains independent and that you move in harmony with the pony's movements.

Exercises without the pony

After the series of exercises in the saddle, we can now do a few exercises without the pony, which we ought to do often. It is very important to remain physically fit to ride well.

These exercises will increase your strength, suppleness and stamina. Many mistakes in a pony/rider combination arise from physical shortcomings in the rider, for example, stiff ankles, stiff loins, lack of stamina, hunched back, stiff shoulders, and so on.

Apart from correcting individual mistakes, you can — by doing these and other exercises — avoid many of the mistakes mentioned. So make sure that you are a fit rider, by doing the following exercises.

The first exercise is rolling the ankle joint. Stand on a cavalletto, which is a wooden pole which rests on X-shaped supports, and lift one foot forward a little. Now let the point of your foot drop and then come up again. Then turn your foot outwards and back again.

Make as large a circle as possible with the point of your foot. This will give you a supple ankle joint, with the result that you will find it easier to hold your heel low and your calf in place. Exercise both ankles evenly.

For the second exercise, sit on the ground with your feet on a cavalletto, then lift your back, supporting yourself on your hands. Do this exercise several times in succession. It will exercise your back muscles and strengthen your shoulder joints which will help you to keep a good upright position on your pony.

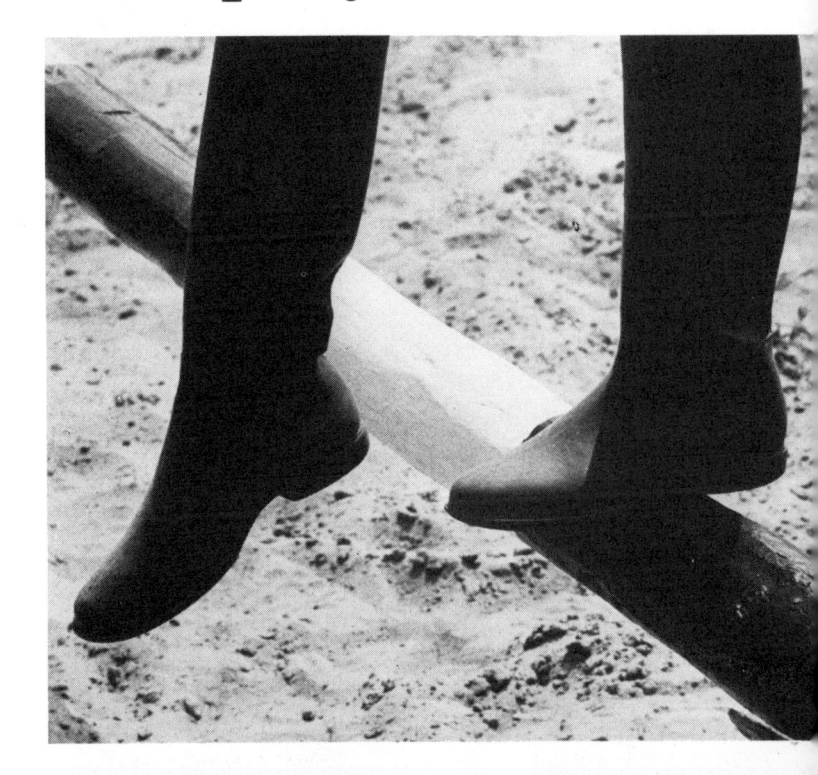

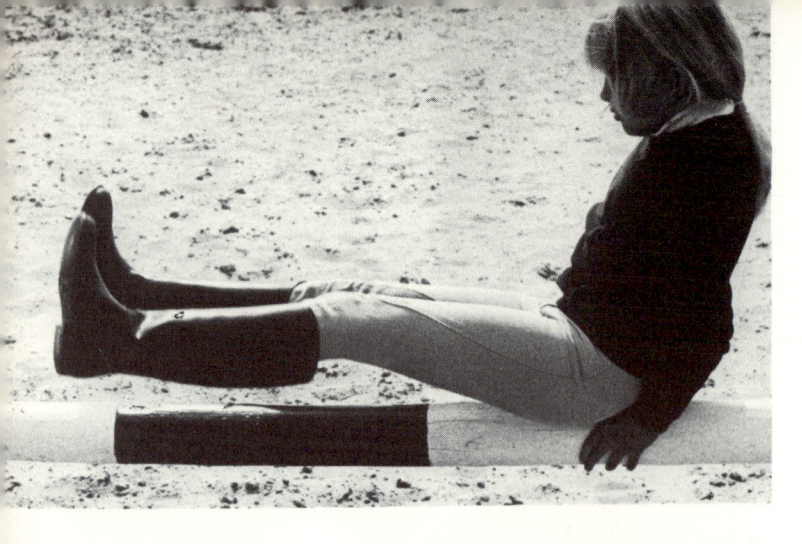

Now sit on the cavalletto with your legs outstretched on either side of it. Support yourself on the cavelletto with your hands behind you. Now try to tap your feet against each other above the cavalletto, then lower then gently. This exercise gives you strong abdominal muscles, which you need in order to follow the movement of the pony's back in the walk, trot and canter.

The next exercise seems somewhat complicated, but it is very good for general stamina and good control of your body. Begin by standing with your feet together and your arms stretched above your head. Then move your legs apart and, at the same time, move your right arm forward and your left arm backward. Then jump back into the initial position, legs together and arms stretched above your head. Now go on, legs apart again, your left arm forward and your right arm backward. Continue doing this with alternate arms.

Now an exercise to give suppleness to the shoulder joint. Stand with your legs apart, holding a riding whip firmly in both hands against your back. Now bend forward and raise the whip. If you do this properly, your shoulders will become supple, which will give you a steady hand – and this is one of the most important things in pony riding.

The loins must be supple in order to be able to do the sitting trot well, as we have seen already. An exercise which helps in this is the following: stand with your legs apart, holding the whip in both hands; your trunk should be held horizontally. Now draw the whip over to the right, at the same time turning your trunk to the right. Do the same thing to the left.

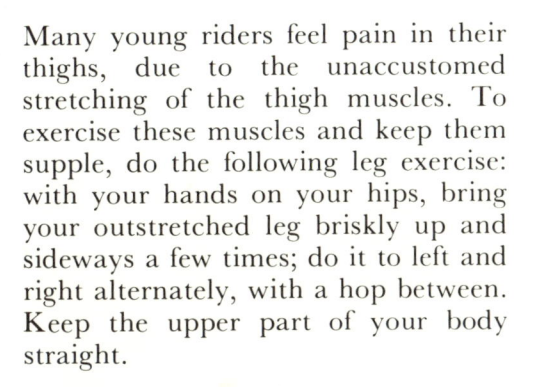

Many young riders feel pain in their thighs, due to the unaccustomed stretching of the thigh muscles. To exercise these muscles and keep them supple, do the following leg exercise: with your hands on your hips, bring your outstretched leg briskly up and sideways a few times; do it to left and right alternately, with a hop between. Keep the upper part of your body straight.

Supporting yourself with your hands on the cavalletto, jump backwards and forwards over it to the left and the right alternately, at the same time moving along the cavalletto from one point to the next. Keep your feet together. This exercise strengthens the muscles of your shoulders and legs.

The next exercise is called winding up the horseshoe. One or more horseshoes are tied to a stick with a cord about 1 metre (just over 1 yard) long. You should take this stick in both hands and quickly wind the cord round the stick, like this. This makes the muscles of your forearm and wrists strong and supple, which is indispensable for good control of the reins.

Bending and stretching your trunk, using the cavalletti. Sit on a cavalletto and stretch out your legs till your feet are underneath a cavalletto opposite. First bend forward with your hands behind your head until your nose touches your knees. Then stretch back again, until you are lying in a horizontal position with your feet still held underneath the other cavalletto. Do this a number of times backwards and forwards. In this way you will strengthen your abdominal muscles and make your back supple.

Swinging the trunk with one leg outstretched sideways exercises the thigh muscles and increases the suppleness of the trunk, which makes for good independence of the seat. Place your left and right leg alternately at hip level on the support of a jump stand, and then swing forward until your fingers touch the ground.

We continue by rocking on our toes on a cavalletto. Stand balanced on a cavalletto. Of course, you can hold on to the edge of the *manège*. Now go up and down on your toes, taking your heels as far down as possible. This strengthens your calf and ankle muscles, which is necessary for good impelling action with your calf and for holding your heels low.

We now come to the last exercise of this chapter: bending your knees and raising a bar or cavalletto. Place one end of a bar of a jump pole or cavalletto on the edge of the *manège* and hold the other end with both hands at chest level. With this heavy load, you now make deep knee bends. This is to strengthen the leg and shoulder muscles.

If you want to train your whole body well and increase your stamina, you can do these last six exercises in the form of 'circuit training'. Do the first exercise for half a minute, then rest for half a minute, then do the next exercise for half a minute, again resting for half a minute, and so on, until you have completed all six exercises. You must keep increasing the number of exercises that you do, adjusting the time you exercise. For example, one minute of exercise, one minute of rest, or one minute of exercise and half a minute of rest.

Of course, this is not the only way you can exercise. You can do all the exercises in this chapter regularly before or after each riding lesson. Good luck!

Index

Aids 74–82
    driving 10, 76
    riding 63, 74, 78

Bails 22
Bandages 37
    applying 38–40
'bars' 9, 43, 50, 77
Bedding 23
Bit 9, 14, 43, 46, 50, 52, 79
Box 15
Bridle 16, 41, 43, 46, 49, 50, 51, 52, 53, 78
Browband 50–1

Cannon 12
Canter 66, 67, 82
Cavalletto 89–95
Certificate of vaccination 20
Cheekpieces 43, 50
Clipping 29–32
    equipment 29
Competitions 38
    dressage 76
Coronet 12
Croup 55, 57
Crupper loop 48
Curry comb 26

Dandy brush 26
Droppings 19

Ears 8, 50
Exercises 83–95
Eyes 8, 23

Farrier 28
Feed 24
Feet 12
Fetlock 12
Field 18–9
Forelock 50–1
Frog 12
    picking out 28

Gaits 66–7
Galls 42, 43, 47, 48
Girth(s) 43, 47, 48, 49, 54, 58, 74
Grooming
    before saddling 47
    kit 25
    procedure 26–8
Gymkhanas 81

Hairs
    mane 33
    tactile 9, 30
    tail 36
Halter 47, 50
Hands 77–82

Head 8
Headcollar 15, 17, 21
Hindquarters 10, 16
Hip 11
Hock 11, 12
Hoof 12
Hoof pick 26
Hooves 26–8
Horsebox 40

Jaws 9

Knee 11, 12
Knot(s)
    for bails 22
    tying up 17

Leg aids 74, 77, 78
Leg protectors 39
Legs 9, 11, 12, 67, 71, 73, 80
    protection 37
Lunging 38

Mane 52, 83
    cleaning 26
    neatening 31
    plaiting 33–5
Manège 73, 82, 94, 95
Martingale(s) 44, 46
Mouth 9, 66, 82
Muscles 11
    back 10

Neck strap 44
Nose 9
Noseband 45, 51–2
Nostrils 9, 51
Numnah 43, 47, 48

Parotid gland 9
Pastern 12
Ponies
    Fjord 31, 33
    Haflinger 31
    Iceland 48, 66
    Welsh 31, 33
Pony games 81
Posture 59, 70, 83
Punishment 14

Rack 66
Reins 15, 44, 46, 50, 52, 54, 56–8, 60, 66, 73, 79, 83
Rein aids 77, 80

Saddle 41, 46, 47, 49, 53, 55, 59, 61, 62, 63, 66, 70, 71, 73, 83, 86
Saddle cantle 42, 54, 61, 87
Saddlecloth, *see* Numnah
Saddle gullet 42, 47

Saddle horse 46
Saddle pommel 42, 54, 57, 86, 87, 89
Schooling 70
Seat 59–63, 77, 80
Shampoo 27
Shelter 18
Shoulder(s) 14, 54, 76
Snaffle(s) 44–5, 50, 51, 77
Sores, *see* Galls
Spinal column 9
Spine 10
Spurs 77
Stable 18, 22–3, 58
Standing 15
Stifle 11
Stirrup irons 46, 47, 48, 54, 55, 56, 59, 60, 61
Stirrup leathers 41, 54, 56
Stirrups 42, 54, 56, 62, 70, 73, 83
Sweat flaps 48, 55

Tack
    choosing 41–5
    cleaning 46
Tail 27, 33
    plaiting 36
    protection 39
    trimming 32
Tail strap 48
Teaching 15–6
Teeth 9
Throat latch 46, 50, 52
Travelling 39–40
Trot 66–7, 82
    rising 71–3
    sitting 70–1, 85
    slow 88

Unsaddling 49

Volt 82

Walk 66, 67
Water 23
Weight aids 80
Whip 76, 77, 91
Withers 54, 55, 57, 59
Worming 20
Worms 19